It Ain't You Babe, A Woman's Guide to Surviving Infidelity and Divorce

Isabelle O'Shea

ISBN: 0-9889-7340-5
ISBN-13: 9780988973404

Dedication

To the women of the world who, in good faith and with an open heart, give their all to their relationships.

Acknowledgements

Thanks to all the women who shared their stories in an effort to help others. Thanks to the attorneys, investigators, physicians and counselors who shared their time and experience in the hope of sparing others pain, mistakes and misfortune.

Special thanks to the magazine editors who published parts of this book because they believed the material would inform and inspire.

Cover artwork by Bonnie Cuddihy

Table of Contents:

Why Read This Book

"This is a down and dirty, practical guidebook for folks who need to understand what is going on with them during divorce and recovery. It's a successful mix of confessional, instructional and inspirational elements all resting on a platform of solid research. The honesty of the author makes this book so much more credible than the more typical "expert's" narrative of "various "do's and don'ts."

Dr. W.R., Psychologist

"This book is a wonderful "how to" story filled with personal insight and universal emotional reactions to an all too familiar life occurrence. The author shares her own vulnerability and reactions with honesty, wit and humor. She couples her personal story with some well researched "academic" opinions and knowledge on a range of relevant topics. This is an inspiring story with lessons that can be applied to many other life-altering events."

C.D., Medical Social Worker

Every divorce is different, and yet it can also be said that every divorce is the same. This author's account of hers captures both qualities—uniqueness and commonality—along with hard-learned lessons to learn from.

GT, Author

Author Bio

The author has changed her name, and the names of others in this book to protect the privacy of all parties. Otherwise, all dialogue and events took place as she remembers them. The author is a licensed certified rehabilitation counselor and former social worker who has published articles relating to health, medicine and lifestyle in numerous regional and national magazines.

Part I
Suspicion

Chapter 1
Along Came a Spider

"Life has its woes so learn to be on your toes, be alert." Bernard Kelvin Clive

The Christmas before my marriage ended, my husband gave me a letter. This letter was inside a beautiful Christmas card, on which medieval angels in gold and royal blue sang, played trumpets and arched their perfect white wings.

On a simple piece of white paper filled with his loopy, scrawling handwriting, he declared his love for me and his happiness with our relationship. "Thank you for all you give me, thank you for your love, thank you for your caring. Thank you for your spirit and vitality and all the energy it gives me, just by hearing your voice—it restores my soul."

It was the type of letter you keep hidden away, so that on a gray, rainy day when you feel a little lost, you can take it out and feel rejuvenated by the memory of someone else's caring. He ended it by saying he looked forward to spending the rest of his life with me.

We had a few rocky times in our marriage of 20 years but the past decade had been so good, so easy, so fun; I thought we were set. Other people often commented on how loving we were, saying, "How lucky you both are." I thought so too.

Rob was dynamic, expressive and charismatic. I was shy and creative but also driven. My energy and support was the wind beneath his wings. My first marriage had been, with the exception of two beautiful children, a disaster of conflicting personalities, styles and goals; a relationship I left with great guilt after years of failed attempts at resolution.

I had been hesitant to jump into my marriage to Rob, but after a few initial difficulties over conflicting ideas about what marriage was, we had been happy together. This partnership was electric, stimulating, and fun.

The January following that lovely Christmas, I left our Virginia home for Boston to be with my brother who had been diagnosed with colon cancer. He suffered from schizophrenia, had been hospitalized for years and was very much alone. He needed surgery and I needed to be there for him.

My husband and I were partners in a business we built together during our 20 years of marriage. He was a successful consultant to business owners and CEOs. Although I felt alone and isolated, I did not want to share the burden of my brother's care with him. I knew how busy he was. I told him I could handle it alone. "Don't worry, I'll be fine."

I wound up staying in Boston for a month, spending my days in the intensive care unit of a hospital and my nights in a nearby hotel room. My brother's mental illness made it much more difficult for him to accept treatment and stabilize following the surgery. Any time I left his room, a nurse had to take my place as he was often delusional and hard to control. It was agony to watch him endure such pain, especially because he could not fully understand what was happening.

During this time I had many tearful phone conversations with my husband. I would have liked him to come—I desperately needed emotional support—but it was in my nature to be the good wife and spare him what I knew would be an awful experience and one that would take him away from his work. During these calls, he would occasionally mention a woman he recently met named Melissa.

He was the primary speaker at a large business conference. At lunch, a woman sat next to him. She had seen him speak, she flattered him, and she asked him to "mentor" her. He agreed. She offered to help him with some of his projects. My husband spoke of her with admiration and praise. He said she was married to an older man in poor health and confided she married him only because he was ill and needed her help. Rob thought this was very kind of her.

My radar was up. I heard the warmth in his voice as he talked about her, but I had no time to wonder about this relationship. I was trying to get my brother through the worst experience of his life.

By February, my brother was stable. I called Rob, who was on his way to New York on business. He casually mentioned that he and Melissa had established an ongoing working relationship, explaining how helpful she was. It was clear she was offering him support, suggestions and most of all, adulation.

We agreed I should fly to New York for the Valentine's Day weekend for a reunion of sorts. Despite the bitter weather I was excited. New York is a stimulating environment, a great change from the sterile interior of the hospital and the anonymous environment of the Comfort Inn I had stayed in for a month.

At first, there was joyfulness as we embraced, but then he seemed to draw away from me. There was an air of uncertainty. He seemed distant and strange, picking at me in an unkind way—not like himself.

As we walked down 42nd street, we were bathed in the warm yellow light that streamed from restaurants and shops. We stopped at Zabar's, a store famous for its wonderful coffee and foods. Every time we went to New York, Zabar's was a favorite stop, but this time things felt different. He looked at things but did not buy, he hardly spoke. I chattered, filling the empty air, attempting to reach him. I could not believe that after being apart for a whole month that our reunion would be so dismal.

Outside, the sidewalks were slick with ice. A freezing wind hit us, making me slide, so I reached out for his arm. He made a slight move away from me, and followed with a sharp remark. I stopped, and without thinking, struck his arm with my fist. We were both stunned as we looked at each other, and we walked back to the hotel in silence, eager to get out of the bitter cold. I knew something had changed, that something deep and sinister was happening to "us." Back in the room, he denied it and apologized. I wanted to talk and he didn't.

During the next few months, I continued flying back and forth from Virginia to Boston. I met with my brother's doctors, took him for radiation treatments, took him out to eat—anything to try to make his life a little happier. When the weather warmed, we would sit in the grass near the hospital and play checkers or reminisce about our childhood years, about the good years before he became ill. He finally recovered from his surgery but did not know that he had only one year to live. I was determined to make that year as good as I could.

I would see my husband on the rare occasions we were both in Virginia. He would talk about his new friend Melissa and their joint projects. He suddenly insisted on putting cucumber slices in his Perrier water because that was what she did. He bought an electric toothbrush and had his teeth whitened. He got a new hairstyle, younger, punkier, with gel—truly a departure in behavior.

At home one morning, I was peeling a hard-boiled egg, flicking the peelings into the trash. Rob came over to me and with a patronizing smile instructed me, "If you would put these under the cold water as soon as they come out of the pan, they would peel much easier." He smiled as he shared this new bit of wisdom with me, obviously pleased with himself. I said, "Rob, that is exactly how I have been cooking the eggs for the last 20 years." On the day he ordered designer jeans tailor-made for him, I felt sure something was going on.

For our wedding anniversary in April we went to Williamsburg, Va., to visit an art gallery and have dinner at the Trellis restaurant, the site of one of our first dates. It was a beautiful spring weekend with new green coming out on the trees, the fragrance of hyacinths in the air, Easter decorations in all the storefronts.

It should have been a joyful event but my husband was clearly distract-ed. During the meal, his cell phone rang constantly. He took every call with obvious excitement and turned away from me or went outside to respond. I asked him to stop. He said "they" were in the middle of some important deals. He seemed obsessed. Over our anniversary dinner, as my duck and his salmon got cold, I leaned forward and asked him, "Are you having an affair?"

Chapter 2
Twenty Signs You Are About to Be Dumped

"Things are going to get a lot worse before they get worse." Lilly Tomlin

You may think I waited a long time before I asked this question out loud, but I had seen him excited about working with other people (men and women) before and we all want to avoid the unthinkable. However, all the signs were there. Sally Warren in her excellent book, *Dumped*[1], points out the following 20 signs you are about to be dumped.

1) Walking down the street, he walks a few steps ahead of you. He acts "muted." Not really making contact.
2) He calls you a lot—so you won't call him.
3) He does not call you at all.
4) He makes calls outside.
5) He checks his cell phone frequently.
6) He is working late a lot or taking business trips he doesn't want to discuss in detail.
7) His business trips are now to new, "different" destinations.
8) No intimate conversations about his feelings, what worries him or what he's thinking about.
9) He is tuned out to you- emotionally not there for you. You begin to second guess everything you say, you try to amuse. He's not into you.
10) He is irritable all the time, with an undercurrent of anger.
11) Sex is over.
12) Or very different—he can suddenly be more passionate.
13) He finds fault with you. (This is typical and very hurtful behavior. If he can make you be at fault then he can leave with less guilt.)
14) He changes: new haircut, new clothes, interest in his appearance, new car or new activities.

15) He does not want to talk about the future.

16) Wrong numbers, phone hang-ups, calls late at night.

17) He encourages your private pursuits, suggests you take a trip, get separated from him.

18) You have a mutual woman friend; he suddenly avoids her, does not want to talk with you about her.

19) When you ask what is wrong, he won't talk, or claims he is under pressure at work.

20) A friend clues you in.

If one or more of these are occurring, it may be in your best interest to find out what is really going on. You may want to skip ahead and take steps listed in Chapter 8—*What to do About It.*

My Wild Imagination

At our anniversary dinner, when I asked him outright whether he was having an affair, I was told, "No, don't be ridiculous, how crazy!" He went on to say that I had such a wild imagination. How could I think that? For the rest of the dinner, he was more animated, more interactive. We went home and he made love to me, but still I felt a distance growing.

That Sunday, he was leaving for a trip. He stood on our front porch, where I said to him, "Rob, would you ever leave me?" He absent-mindedly touched my breast and said, "No, no honey. You are sooo convenient."

Convenient? I was convenient? I do not think he even knew he said it. He would be away again, this time for two weeks, and yes, he would be working with Melissa. "She is invaluable."

His return flight landed at 11:30 p.m. on a Friday night. I met his plane at the airport as I had done almost every week for the past 20 years. He was running a fever and was delirious. While in Texas, he was bitten by a tick, and the bite was infected. His calf had a massive red wound. He was babbling and trying to get messages off his phone. I literally had to support him to get him to the car.

"Melissa, Melissa, Melissa…I have to get Melissa's call. Melissa called; I have to get her message."

This went on all the way home. He refused a trip to the emergency room. "No, no, I'll be fine. We will go in the morning."

The next morning, I took him to the emergency room. The doctor took one look and gasped, "This is a real mess!" He asked me to hold Rob's leg still and immediately cut open his wound, carving out a fist of dead tissue.

The doctor said, "You got here just in time." My husband was admitted to the hospital.

As he became coherent, Rob asked me to go home and get his laptop and a list of other files and supplies. When I returned to his hospital room, he got a call, pulled himself out of the bed and in front of the astonished nurse, limped down the hall, limping away to take the call in private. Questioning him was futile. He denied that there was anything else or anyone else. It was clear to me there was.

Shock

After my husband recovered from his leg surgery, he left for New York on another "business trip." He still denied any romantic involvement with Melissa. That night I did something I had never done before: I went into his email account. I felt terrible doing this behind his back, but what I found devastated me.

There were emails, piles of emails between the two of them. They expressed their lust for each other and described trysts they had had, including their "first incredible kiss." He described her naked body. Worst of all, I read her suggestion that he leave me, that I was holding him back. She literally said that women my age did not like sex, only chocolate. She said, "She wants the marriage to be over, she just cannot tell you." Clearly, they had a history that went back several months. She wrote passages full of sexual suggestion, his complete acceptance, their plans for experiences together—all under the guise of business trips.

I started at 10 p.m. and downloaded email until 4 a.m. I was shaking; my heart beat was out of sync, throbbing in my chest. The more I read, the worse it became. I could not breathe, adrenalin surged through my veins, making it hard to form a coherent thought. I went into the bathroom and vomited, trying to get rid of the bad news I had taken in. Then I picked up the phone.

I called Rob's cell, my hands shaking so badly I could not hit the numbers. He answered half asleep.

He said, "Uh, uh….. I have to take this outside."

I said, "Why, why do you have to take it outside? Is someone with you? She is there isn't she? She is there in bed with you. Right?"

At first he denied it. Then he admitted it. I read him one of the emails. He was silent.

I said, "What does this mean?"

He said, "I love you, but I love her too."

I dropped the phone, sobbing. I left the house and got into the car, driving mindlessly through darkness, sobbing and choking, hoping a tractor trailer would hit me and put me out of my misery.

At 6 a.m. I called him again and said, "Rob, please, please, come home."

"Oh no, I have clients here. I have appointments to keep."

"I don't care. You must come home now. I will call her home and speak with her husband if you don't."

He said, "Don't do that. No don't do that. Her husband has leukemia. You'll kill him if you call him." He agreed to come home.

Chapter 3
Your Situation

"I have a new mantra, which I chant softly to myself: 'Oh My God Oh My God.'" Suzanne Finnamore[2]

To *suspect* your spouse is having an affair is troubling, but when you see the absolute evidence and can no longer live in denial, the impact is terrible. When I saw the evidence of my husband's infidelity and heard him acknowledge that he was in love with another person, it threw me into a state of physical and emotional shock. It was excruciatingly painful. I was the walking wounded, hardly able to function, not coherent, weeping and broken. I think back to some of the conversations I had then and believe that people must have thought me insane.

If this happens to you, you too may be in shock. Try your best not to do what I did. Try not to let your spouse know that you suspect an affair or know he is having an affair. You need more information first. You need time to think about what kind of outcome you want. And even if you are not sure you want to stay in your marriage, it is critical to get legal advice before you talk with your spouse about your suspicions. If you try to save your marriage and fail in the attempt, you will at least know your rights and options.

To refrain from speaking to your spouse about his affair may be the hardest and most counter-intuitive thing you have ever done. You may go without eating or sleeping, you may become anorexic, your heart may race out of control—as mine did—to the point where you are sure you are having a heart attack. You are at one of the lowest points in your life, but you must hold it together and take action now. You can cry your heart out later. Every attorney I spoke with said, "The people who come out best are those who can think out strategy and make plans." So be cool, set your emotions aside, and deal with them when you can.

This is a time to quickly create a support system. You need a counselor and an attorney, plus a few confidants (people whose advice and remarks you respect.) A counselor is important because it will keep you from burning out your friends and your attorney. Steer clear of people who are highly emotional or judgmental. They may push you to take actions not in your best interest.

Dealing with fear and paralysis

Stacy Schneider, attorney and author of the logic-based book, *He had it Coming*,[3] provides the following ways to deal with the emotional turmoil of a marriage or relationship gone bad: First, stop and step back from your thoughts. Try to isolate the negative statements in your head so you can analyze their validity. To analyze without bias, pretend this was happening to a friend of yours. Speak to yourself as you would speak to her. Provide words of support. Then use your inner voice to conduct a similar positive dialogue with yourself that contradicts negative thoughts.

When you go to see an attorney, bring a friend for moral support and to help ask questions and take notes. Before taking action, take a deep breath and count to ten. Write it out. Get your emotions out and onto paper. Create a diary. Try not to make any important decisions now. At the very least, sleep on it or get away to gain a new perspective.

And if tempted to reach out to him, ask yourself, what can you accomplish? Are you trying to get his attention, get him back or lash out in anger? Will any of these things help you in the long run? Overrule your emotions with logic. Stop, pause, and think.

Cindy Patterson, who has 25 years experience as a police officer and ten more in her current career as an investigator in Richmond, Va., said: "I must be very careful about how I give my findings to my clients. It is emotionally devastating to them and they can go off the deep end in many ways." Interestingly enough, she said, "Men are saner in their reactions. They are more concerned about money, not emotions. Your spouse is dealing from logic and you from emotion. Women are in more pain." She added, "Get your head and heart in sync. If your heart is determining your actions, try to get your head and logic to catch up with your emotions. It may take time to adjust."

Dramatic Ways to Receive the Bad News.

A couple I know, Sheila and Steve, were going through what they called, "a bad patch." Sheila knew her husband had had an affair and she felt estranged from him. Wanting some comfort of her own, she began having an affair with his best friend, Dave, who was also married. Dave became very involved. So much so, that he told Sheila he loved only her. She believed him and felt the only honest thing to do would be to tell the spouses when they were all together.

They all went out to dinner one night at a restaurant they frequented as a foursome. At the end of the meal, as they were all sipping their after-dinner liqueurs, she announced the affair to all present. Sheila said she and Dave wanted divorces so they could be married. Everyone's jaw dropped, including her lover—whom she had neglected to forewarn of this announcement. Her husband, her lover and his wife were all blindsided. Dave did not leave his wife. Sheila wound up staying with her husband. Needless to say they did not go out to dinner as a foursome again.

Deborah went to pick up some film that had been developed. It was under her husband's name. She thought she was getting the photos of her daughter's birthday party. Instead, she was treated to a series of shots of her husband and his girlfriend in the nude, experimenting with some rather disgusting poses. She sent him packing and did not even give him the photos.

Marie was contacted by her boyfriend's ex-wife, who asked whether she knew they were sleeping together. When Marie said she did not believe her, the ex-wife suggested Marie check his text messages. Marie learned some great new sexting shorthand and discovered the ex-wife was telling the truth.

Chapter 4
The Joke's on Me

"Deceiving others, that is what the world calls a romance." Oscar Wilde

The morning following my discovery of Rob's emails, Melissa sent an email directly to me. She said "it was all a joke." That email I asked about was done in jest—nothing for me to worry about. She actually said I should trust her.

I sent her the one in which my husband described her naked body. This time there was no reply.

I wanted desperately to reach out to the husband, the cuckolded, innocent husband. I needed him to know too. But the thought that it might be too much for him stopped me. I believed he was sick, as I had seen emails mixed in about his treatments with details that would have been too hard to manufacture. I had had a cousin with leukemia whose cheating husband hastened her death, so I held back.

For the next seven days, I was in a state of physical shock. My heart continued to race wildly like an accelerator stuck in the down position. I could not eat or sleep. My adrenalin was on high. I drove to the YMCA early in the morning while it was still dark, then I sat in my car in the parking lot waiting for it to open at sunrise. I could not focus on anything. All I could do was run, run, run on the indoor track at speeds I had never run before for more miles than I had ever run before as though I could outrun everything that had happened and spin the clock backward to December when he had written me that wonderful letter.

I became an anorexic wonder-woman. I could not stop losing weight. After a week, my heart still raced out of control day and night. I went to a cardiologist who diagnosed me with a condition called "broken heart syndrome." He said that sudden emotional stress can result in severe but reversible heart muscle weakness that mimics a classic heart attack.

Patients with this condition, also called stress cardiomyopathy, are often misdiagnosed as having suffered a massive heart attack, when actually they have suffered from a day- or days-long surge in adrenalin (epinephrine) and other stress hormones that temporarily "stun" the heart. He explained that these chemicals can be temporarily toxic to the heart, effectively stunning the muscle and producing symptoms similar to a typical heart attack, including chest pain, fluid in the lungs, shortness of breath and heart failure.

As my husband and I talked, he said, "When you cry, I want to stay with you. When you are angry I want to go." But he would not stay off the phone with her. Melissa called constantly, trying to insure he would not leave their relationship. She was 15 years younger than my husband. She made him feel young again.

I found out he had made her a legal partner in an entirely new business. Checks came to the house addressed to her; checks from clients who were our business clients from the business my husband and I owned together. His income was now flowing into her pocket and I was soon to be disenfranchised from the business as well as from my husband.

More information came out. They had a secret post office box in which she sent him materials she did not want me to see. They called it their "secret garden." This had a particularly hurtful twist as we had seen that movie together, and loved it so much that he had given me a copy of the book. He had sent her a copy of the same book. Another thing that had been ours was now theirs. Secret Garden is a story about innocence. There was nothing innocent about this secret garden. Descriptions in their messages to each other were salacious.

One of the items in the "secret" post office box was a book by Erica Jong, filled with lusty descriptions of sexual encounters. Melissa actually said in a note that she wanted my husband to read *Any Woman's Blues* as an example of clear, concise reading so they could improve the quality of the newsletter they would write for their new business. I asked him, "Are you so naïve that you did not see this as her attempt to get you thinking sexually about her? Did you not think this was part of a seduction on her part?"

Our business had a Web site. I had helped design it and written copy for it, plus worked with our secretary to get it up and running. Now I found they had a new Web site for *their* business. On the home page was a picture of them together. He was seated; she stood behind him, her arms resting possessively on his shoulders. She was short with blond hair, a slim body. Two of my friends said she looked like me, but younger. I could not bear the sight of her hands on his shoulders.

My dislike of her turned to hatred when I read what she had written to my husband about me, urging him to leave. And although I knew she was an accomplished liar and cheated on her own husband, something about her direct email assuring me I had blown "a joke" out of proportion was the element that most fueled my fury.

According to the experts I consulted later, the biggest mistake I made at the time was to let my husband know I was aware of his affair before I knew what I wanted to do about it.

Part II
Why?

Chapter 5
You, Me and Christie Brinkley

"The only way for a man to be rid of his old self is to see his new self-mirrored in the eyes of some woman." Clare Booth Luce

What do you and I have in common with Christie Brinkley, Jennifer Aniston, Halle Berry, Debbie Reynolds, Jackie Onassis, Hilary Clinton, Ivana Trump, Barbara Walters, Elin Nordegren, Sandra Bullock and Martha Stewart? They all are beautiful, smart, successful and were probably wonderful wives. They were all cheated upon by their husbands—every one of them. What does that tell you?

Lovely Christie Brinkley said she learned of her husband's affair when the stepfather of a teenage girl approached her and told her that her husband was fooling around with his daughter and would not stop. One glance at her husband's face revealed the man was telling her the truth. She thought, "Oh my God, he did that!" She turned to her husband and said, "How could you?[4]" Two years earlier, he had begun to ignore her and rebuff her attempts to be intimate.

Gorgeous Ivana Trump, with her sexy Hungarian accent, was lauded as an extraordinary manager of Donald Trump's huge hotels in New York. She had her husband's mistress follow them to Vail, where a public scene on the slopes ensued. She demanded that this woman leave her husband alone, but that is not what happened.

Jennifer Aniston, everyone's ideal of the girl next door, had to learn she was losing the love of her life, Brad Pitt, by reading the tabloids.

Martha Stewart had just published her first best-selling book on the perfect bucolic lifestyle—a book she dedicated to her husband—when she found he was having a heated affair with her own administrative assistant.

Hilary Clinton, who dedicated much of her life to her husband's career, is possibly the most publicly humiliated woman in American history as the press, plus every late-night comedian, ridiculed Bill Clinton's escapades with Monica Lewinsky.

Elin Nordregen, the lovely blonde Swedish model, was cheated on by her husband, Tiger Woods, (who we all thought was a really, really good guy) so many times that we lost count.

Halle Berry, gorgeous Bond girl and Catwoman, wanted to die after her baseball player husband cheated on her repeatedly.

Sandra Bullock, a woman known for her street smarts, was shocked to find her devoted husband, Jessie James, had been carrying on multiple affairs with various tattooed ladies and had managed to keep it secret for years despite their high-profile lives.

Debbie Reynolds has a particularly interesting story. She suffered the ignominy of losing two husbands who were cheaters. Her first husband, Eddie Fisher, left her for Elizabeth Taylor. In doing so, he left her with the comforting statement that he had never really loved her. He never came to visit his two children again. Her second husband, Harry Karl, took her to the cleaners after losing his own fortune. He even hocked her jewelry. In an ironic and bitter twist, she wound up having to pay off half of his debts.

She said, "My car broke down in front of the club we had gone to every week for years. I walked there and asked to use the phone. They would not allow me inside because Harry still had his membership there. I had to walk to a house and ask to use their phone." [5] This happened while she was living wherever she could find a bed and continuing to pay off his bills with her nightclub routine.

Chapter 6
It Ain't You, Babe

"The search for a scapegoat is the easiest of all hunting expeditions."
Dwight D. Eisenhower

I was recently at the beach with a girlfriend of mine who was watching a beautiful, high-profile woman on TV. Her husband, even more famous than she, had been caught cheating. It was all over the news. My friend said, "You know she must have been a bitch for him to cheat on her so much."

I levitated off the floor and listed a litany of women, both famous and familiar—including my friend *herself*—who had been cheated on by their spouses. She said, "Oh yeah, you are right."

It is a common misconception that when a man cheats, it must be his wife's fault. If it has happened to you, you know better. My ex-husband, to his credit, never blamed me. He said, "It ain't you babe, it's just that I was so stagnant in my life."

Who could beat Jackie Kennedy Onassis as the perfect wife? No one. But being the toast of foreign countries and one of the country's most beloved first wives was not enough to protect her from her husband's cheating. The answer is no matter how much you do, how good you look, how talented, smart or charming you are, you too can find yourself made a fool of.

Now, you may intellectually agree with the above passage, but if you were raised in a conservative, old-school environment, or if (like me) you are Catholic or Jewish—both of which are guilt and neurosis-laden faiths—you will invariably feel in your gut that you must have done something to deserve this.

The likelihood is that it has nothing to do with you. Your spouse may attempt to make you think it was your fault for two reasons. First, he does not want to accept blame, not from himself, or from you or from others. And secondly, for him to emotionally separate himself from you he must make you a negative, an object of anger, pity, scorn or guilt. That makes it easier for him to break away from you emotionally.

You may have observed this kind of "picking on the spouse" behavior in associates. When you see this happening, it could mean the bullying spouse is having an affair or about to desert his spouse. It is simply a psycho-logical tool to make it easier to disassociate so he feels like he's not the bad guy.

Women have historically been held responsible, both by men and un-fortunately by other women, for things going wrong in the world. If a child is misbehaving, if a child has psychological problems, the mother is held up for examination. In this country, as recently as the '60s, children who showed signs of a serious mental illness such as schizophrenia or bi-polar or a devel-opmental disorder such as autism (all now known to be biological diseases) were thought to have been "mothered" incorrectly. In Puritan times, if any-thing went wrong—from a disease epidemic to cows going dry—women were accused of being witches and blamed.

In some Muslim societies, if a woman is seen wearing anything except a black tent, she is accused of "enticing" men. Similarly, in other societies, when a female is raped it is she who is blamed, even if she is a child. Women who are unfaithful have historically received harsher punishments than men. Even today, in some countries, it is permissible that a woman be stoned to death for adultery (but not the men.) The sad part is that other women buy into these perspectives that keep their own sex in the position of being the fall guy for whatever bad things men do. Does the term "double-standard" ring a bell?

So, when a man is unhappy in his marriage or when he feels the need to screw around, it is his wife who will be looked at cross-eyed, not him. Again, look at the numerous cases I put forth earlier of perfectly lovely wom-en who tried their best to keep their men happy and still their husbands were unfaithful.

The drive to be unfaithful coupled with men's and society's acceptance of a lack of commitment is what is wrong—not your bedroom technique, not the negligee you wear, nor your hairstyle or makeup. It is important to do your best, whether you be man or woman, to make your spouse happy. Cheating should not be a solution for either of you.

Problems can be solved through talking, counseling, separation and perhaps divorce, but not through cheating. As Dr. Joyce Hudson, a counselor with 30 years of experience in both relationship counseling and sex therapy, said: "the cheated-on spouse must not take responsibility for his partner's actions. You cannot be so bad that you force a spouse to cheat nor can you be so good that you stop a spouse from cheating." If you are unhappy, the options you have are (1) discussion with your mate (2) counseling (3) separa-tion (4) divorce. Cheating should not be an option.

So I would say that if he is unhappy, if he wants to talk, suggests counseling or is thinking divorce, maybe it's you. But if he is cheating? It's him.

Is It Neglect?

"Martyrs of a sort were men and women hastening to adulterous trysts, risking disgrace and divorce for their fix of motel love, all sacrificing the outer world for the inner proclaiming with this priority that everything seeming solid and substantial is in fact a dream of less account than a merciful rush of feeling..." writes John Updike in the book *Witches of Eastwick.*

Given that a man can have the perfect wife—beautiful, loving, smart and successful—why would he risk everything? His home, his children, his fortune, his career, his political stature?

M. Gary Neuman[6], who was featured on the Oprah show, answers that question this way:

"What's the number one reason men cheat? Ninety-two percent of men said it wasn't primarily about the sex. The majority said it was an emotional disconnection, specifically a sense of feeling under-appreciated. A lack of thoughtful gestures," Gary said. "Men are very emotional beings, they just don't look like that. Or they don't seem like that. Or they don't tell you that."

With daily worries such as bills, children and chores, Gary says it's easy for couples to drift away from appreciating one another the way they should. Gary says the other woman often makes the man feel better about himself. "She makes them feel different. Makes them feel appreciated, admired," he said. "Men look strong, look powerful and capable. But on the inside, they're insecure like everybody else. They're searching and looking for somebody to build them up to make them feel valued."

All of this is true Gary, and that's why marriages often fail. However, cheating is a whole different story. Did Tiger Woods have to sleep with 121 different women to feel appreciated? And Jessie James? He evidently needed to have ongoing affairs with strip artists and tattoo models because they provided him with the "thoughtful gestures" he wasn't getting at home. Do we think the difference between Jennifer Aniston and Angelina Jolie was that Angelina was more thoughtful and considerate than Jennifer?

Not to say there are not men (and women) who get into an affair because they feel neglected or even emotionally abused. That happens. But a look at your media of choice shows so many people repeatedly cheating that the term "sex addiction" has been coined. Is there such a thing? I do not know. But if there is, no one has found a cure.

Is it Biology?

Some say that infidelity is natural. They point out that many animals have harems: deer, monkeys, lions, etc. In fact, most of the animal population tends to stray, have several partners or change partners routinely. But it is also true that some animals are monogamous: geese, some species of antelope, swans, wolves, eagles and beavers, to name a few. But we are not like most animals. While the human male has a biological imperative to spread his genetic material around, the human female has a need to nest and she needs a faithful mate to help raise their children.

In nature, male animals that are polygamous must fight off all competitors. If they lose the battle, the new male comes in and mates with all the females. Often, he will kill the offspring of his former rival.

To apply nature's rules to human society, you would have men struggling to support huge families or to support several separate families. Their resources, time, emotions and finances would be spread too thin. Children would not receive sufficient psychological and financial support. And, if we really copied nature, the strongest, most aggressive males would drive off other husbands, seize their women and abandon their children or worse.[7] Fortunately, we have laws to try to prevent this kind of social chaos.

But despite our laws and traditions, the divorce rate is rising and many men find themselves struggling to support two or more families. When they are unable to do this, they often abandon their first family. Also, many men and women become step-parents whether they want to or not. The step parent may have a hard time relating to the step-children and vice versa. They may completely reject one another.

The high rate of divorce also leads parents to move both geographically and emotionally away from their biological children. Parents with the best intentions find it difficult to provide emotional support to their young once they move out of the house, and more so if they move a long distance away. Basically, following a biological sexual imperative is disastrous for society.

Is it Addiction?

Is there such a thing as sex addiction, or is that just a new excuse for bad behavior? The standard manual for psychiatrists and psychologists, the *Diagnostic and Statistical Manual* or *DSM-IV-TR*, while not specifying sexual addiction as a condition, does include a miscellaneous diagnosis called *Sexual Disorders Not Otherwise Specified,* which now includes: "distress about a pattern of repeated sexual relationships involving a succession of lovers who are experienced by the individual only as things to be used." That is an interesting defining line: a person who uses other people as though they were *things.*

Ian Kerner, Ph.D., sex therapist, counselor and author of the book *Sex Detox: A Program to Detoxify and Rejuvenate Your Love Life,* believes "there are growing numbers of people who find themselves in the grip of compulsive sexual behaviors that are beyond their control; behaviors that seriously damage their lives as well as those of their loved ones."

Most therapists seeing patients for this problem see the Internet as a driving force for developing an addiction to pornography because of the speed, availability and low cost of images. These images, accessible at work, at home, and even on your cell phone, have created havoc for managers, parents and spouses. The availability of continuous images that reinforce the gratification of pornography speeds the addictive process.

Does an addiction to pornography lead one to act out these images? Does it lead to addictive sexual acts? I don't think the research is in yet, but my personal guess would be yes.

Actor David Duchovney portrayed a sex-addicted writer in the T.V. series *Californication.* Shortly after, he admitted he was going into a rehabilitation program for sex addiction. Sex, like drugs, alcohol and gambling, triggers pleasure centers in the brain that then demand more of the same.

While some therapists define sexual addiction as a situation in which the addict begins to use others as though they were objects, other therapists define a sex addict as a person who cannot control his impulses and indulges in repetitive behavior that affects his personal life, relationships and/or work and is willing to risk any kind of punishment and loss to continue—including losing relationships and committing crimes. Peter Cook, (Christie Brinkley's ex) admitted in court to lurid tales about his sexual activities which, he felt, were a form of addiction.

A girlfriend of mine named Shelly, in her twenties and gorgeous, was swept off her feet by an elegant, romantic man who seemed quite the catch. He had been married twice before and had plausible stories about why those marriages did not work out. They had a wonderful courtship, traveled extensively together and seemed destined for a marriage made in heaven.

But, soon after the wedding was over, his behavior changed. He began to want sex several times a day, talked obsessively about it, and even on days when they had sex, he masturbated numerous times. He became very controlling about what she wore, her activities and her time. After a year of trying to find a way to help him or change his behavior, she bolted. It was way too much.

Hearing an extreme story like this makes you believe there are some who truly have a sexual addiction, not just to porn, but to literally acting out fantasies and obsessions with partners. But this is not the behavior of the typical straying married male.

Is it Predatory Women?

When I was six years old, my parents took my brother and I on a trip to Florida. We stayed at a motel with palm trees, a big pool, a cage with parrots and even a statue of a zebra in front of the motel. I thought it was incredibly exotic.

My father was a handsome man. He had been a boxer, a lifeguard and was then a policeman. On our second day there, he was by the pool preparing to dive. A woman in a sexy bathing suit slinked over and began a conversation with him. I was only six. I had no ideas about sex, infidelity or any such things, but something about that woman disturbed me. She was too warm; too smiley and standing much too close to him. I had no idea why; but this made me furious.

I thought of my mother resting in the motel room, unaware of this little drama. I was a shy child but I was emboldened by my rage. I went up to them, pushed her out of the way and said loudly, "Mommy needs you to come to the room, right now!" They both looked at me and laughed. I stamped my foot and said, "RIGHT NOW!" So, he excused himself and went back to the motel room.

I followed him, pausing once to give her the dirtiest of looks I could muster on my chubby face. My parents repeated this story for years and years. My mother was very pleased.

So, I guess that, in my gut, I have always known they were out there, these predatory women, just waiting to get their claws on another woman's husband or boyfriend. But growing up, dating, through my first young marriage, I don't remember seeing the quantity of these women I see now, nor do I remember their current lack of fear and propriety.

There seems to be an atmosphere of shamelessness now; an "every woman for herself" attitude. Growing up, did we ever hear stories about women trying to kill their married lover's wives? Not that I recall. But we do now. Ask Mary Jo Buttafuoco, who was shot in the face by her husband's

16-year-old lover. Men tell me, "They are out there. They are everywhere, just ready to do whatever you want."

Rielle Hunter ambushed John Edwards outside his hotel and cornered him long enough to tell him how "hot" she found him. She schemed to get a job with his campaign by offering free video work and then proceeded to seduce him, disregarding his wife's close presence.

When "queen of mean" Leona Helmsley, of Helmsley Hotel fame, learned of Harry Helmsley's real estate holdings and fortune, she set out to take him away from his wife of 33 years, Eve. Leona got herself hired by Harry's real-estate firm, and initiated repeated contacts with Harry, doting on him, flirting with him and impressing him with false stories about her talents and lifestyle.

Once she had him involved sexually, she pushed for him to leave his wife despite his repeated statements that he would never leave his wife because he loved and respected her. As he resisted, she concocted a fantasy lover who she claimed had proposed and who she would marry unless he left Eve. Her tactic worked and she became Mrs. Harry Helmsley.

Steve, my blue collar friend, was a supervisor in a manufacturing plant. He was repeatedly propositioned by several female employees. They knew he was married, and they did not care. They may have wanted to gain leverage or favors. Had he been in a peer position with them, my guess is that the number of offers would have been dramatically less.

Women compete with one another, especially on the job, and the seduction of a man with perceived power adds to their own sense of status. Men tend more to be team players. They tend to respect another man's turf. Or, perhaps they are afraid of what they think is the rightful consequence of screwing with someone else's woman: a thorough beating by the offended male.

Men also seem to have a "don't fool with your best friend's wife" deal, but how many times do we hear from a grieving woman, "I found out he was having an affair with my *best* friend."

Reports indicate that the number of women cheating has increased along with the number of men cheating. Women in the marketplace may have a different view of things. They have learned to be independent and aggressive.

My friends who are dating seem willing to put up with a lot from men. I think that is because women outnumber men, and competition for a man is stiff. It is an era of instant gratification and of the belief that we should all have everything we want when we want it. It is an era of "cougars," older women, married or not, on the prowl.

Is it Changes in our Culture?

Changes in public attitude about infidelity may be another reason men are cheating more often. Statistics show that one-half of all marriages will probably end in divorce if the current frequently quoted rate continues at its present clip.[8]

At one time, American culture publicly opposed infidelity and divorce. Individuals who were perceived as "home wreckers" paid a price, legally, financially and perhaps most importantly, socially. Women's magazines have gone from titles like *Good Housekeeping* to *Self*.

Recently, a huge billboard featuring headless, blown up torsos with a woman's deep cleavage and a man's bare chest was put up by a Chicago law firm.[9] The billboard advised the public in a bold headline: "Life is short, get a divorce!" No mention was made of anyone else's welfare, such as their children's for example. The ad was taken down after numerous complaints but the fact that it could be put up in public at all illustrates just how unimportant the destruction of families and life partnerships is now considered.

Stolen from that motto is the tagline for a Web site called *Ashley Madison*, which, mimicking the Chicago billboard, suggests that "Life is short, have an affair." The Web site guarantees to hook you up with another attached person so you can both have a "discreet" affair. Not only that, but the Web site proudly brags that it has been discussed on multiple mainstream T.V. shows such as Dr. Phil, the View, Larry King, and Ellen. Unbelievable.

In the past, women like Marla Maples, Rielle Hunter and Monica Lewinski would have been vilified. But Monica Lewinski, who shook the stability of her own country by seducing the president, was not labeled a monster but rather given a position as spokesperson for a nationally famous diet food company. Marla Maples, who stole Donald Trump from Ivana, wound up on the cover of *Vogue*. These women, who in a former century might have been shunned, now enjoy 15 minutes of fame.

A Gallup poll completed in May 2008 shows that people's feelings regarding divorce have changed radically in the past few years. In May 2001, Gallup reported that 59 percent of Americans accepted divorce as morally acceptable, but by May 2008, that rate jumped to 70 percent who found it acceptable.[10]

I asked Andrea Stiles, a Richmond, VA attorney with 28 years experience in family law, about the state of judicial attitude toward divorce. She commented, "Yes, the attitude toward divorce has radically changed. When I was young, a divorce was a truly scandalous happening and now it is so commonplace, it hardly raises eyebrows." She thought this was because adultery was more commonplace, or at least perceived as more mundane. She said, "New, young judges will still punish adultery, but older, more experienced judges do not because they have seen so much of it. They are jaded."

Is it the Need to Feel Young Again?

In the movie "Moonstruck," Cher's mother is dealing with her husband's (of forty years) adulterous affair. She goes on a quest for several weeks, asking various people why it is that men cheat. She finally concludes and confides to Cher in a heart-to-heart talk that what she has discovered is that they are afraid of death.

Certainly, this fits the mid-life crisis model. The middle-aged man, realizing he is on the other side of his life, that the glass not half-full any more but now is half-empty, draining away more of his life's precious wine by the day, is delighted to find a young woman flirting with him or responding to his attentions. With her, he can show the world and most importantly himself, that she accepts him as healthy, young, and physically fit enough to be her suitor. He is proud of having out-competed men of her age.

She reminds him of teen love. More than that, she allows him to reenact teen love. How many of these almost over-the-hill guys gleefully remark, "I feel like a teenager again." Yes, teenagers who have little sense of whom they really are and are hormone-driven to throw caution, care and responsibility to the wind.

In my own husband's life, this was clearly part of the deal. He was so very proud of his girlfriend's age (17 years younger) that he mentioned it often. He was blissfully unaware of what a deep, painful cut it made in me each time he said it.

Louise DeSalvo, in her book *Adultery*, writes, "I realized then that adultery is very adolescent. It's when a grown person tries to feel the way they did when they were in high school. Knowing this though, did not help my circumstances at all, for I knew the addictive pleasure of adolescent sex."[11]

Several years ago, I went on a cruise with a girlfriend. We danced each night in one of the ship's clubs. We met an older man (sixties?) who showed up each night, obviously enamored of my friend. I would guess there was at least a 15-year difference between them.

Alone with her, he confided that he had been married for 30 years. His wife was a fine woman, but they had married when both were in college because she became pregnant. The marriage had obviously been a good one. They had two more children together, raised them together, and these children were now successfully on their own.

But, he wondered, had he made a mistake? Was there perhaps more to life than just this? To this end he had begun dance lessons—clearly not just to learn to dance, but to check out the availability of other women.

His wife was on the cruise. We saw her later with him. He did not say hello to us when he was with her. I met her by accident and had a chance to get to know her a little. She was lovely; lovely in body, face and spirit. She clearly did not know what he had on his mind. She thought he wanted to be able to dance with her when they went out together, as a surprise for her, to bring them closer together.

Obviously, this nice woman, who held her husband's hand when they were together, who hugged him and smiled beautifully into his face, was about to get a surprise—and not a good one. My friend, who does not date married men, nixed his approaches but bought his story that his life might be missing something. One of the things it was missing was risk.

Is it the Thrill of Risk?

In her memoir *Perfection*, Julie Metz describes discovering, after her young husband's unexpected death by aneurism, that he had numerous affairs, all thoroughly documented in his computer email. One affair was carried on for several years with one of her close friends who was also married. She is devastated. She goes on her own search for answers. She contacts every woman in the email list and calls them out. Amazingly, she begins a dialogue with two of them and they become friends (sort of).

She goes to her husband's counselor, who is also her own counselor, and asks the question, "Why?" The counselor said, "The last time I saw him, he paused before he left the office, hand on doorknob and said, 'I have come to the conclusion that my life's purpose is risk.'"[12]

The risk of it all—the excitements, the danger, the taboo of the affair—all are extra added attractions. The first-person essay below clearly points that out.

Chapter 7
In Their Own Words

"Women might be able to fake orgasms. But men can fake a whole relationship." Sharon Stone

The Real Reason Men Cheat
Below are excerpts from a very arrogant and selfish, but also frank, essay on why men cheat, written by a married cheater. This anonymous essay appeared in *Esquire* magazine in March 2010. It may turn your stomach but you need to know how some men think.

"This is the most absolute choice I can make. I am there on my own. Against every code, rule, and set of mores I pretend to obey. Against better judgment, against every lesson of hindsight and every shard of wisdom that comes with age, I have no regrets in that moment, because I am naked, or without pants, and I have chosen to be there. I have voted by my presence, declared it, and I feel the blood moving in me again. So it's the blood. That's who I am. That's why men cheat."

Here he is saying- it's the blood- it's in my blood. OK, that is the animal part of him and he enjoys letting it run free. What's wrong with that? As I said before- if you let biology rule unrestrained, you have very nasty social consequences. The whole structure of western civilization and religion is based on rules that keep us from eating each other alive. There are consequences to free love, like children without parents, disabled spouses left to fend for themselves, men or women trying to manage the expense and emotional needs of several families, not to mention murderous acts of jealousy, rage and revenge. There are good reasons, that from Moses' time on, adultery has been a bad idea for society.

The author goes on to explain that in his experience there are no consequences.

"But by and large, infidelity is remarkably easy to hide. More often than not—more often than any man will admit—there is absolutely no consequence. So yes, that freedom exists. A man can." We all know that while, yes, many people can carry out a dual life- in most cases, it eventually be-

comes a public event with all the nasty pain, anger and emotional destruction infidelity causes to the people related to the adulterers.

"If you cheat, you must believe this much: that fated love is a lie,

and monogamous love a deception. If you cheat, these two sentiments are your guiding light." Give me a break- there are numerous great monogamous marriages. By and large, those folks, while maybe not having the excitement in their life that adultery brings, have had happy, productive and contented existences.

"At home, I am attentive to the needs of my marriage. It is a

kind of test, and men need tests. Fidelity is a test that pits a man against his own instincts, urges him to ignore his opportunities, to muffle any sense of expansion." He sees the difficulty of being "attentive to the needs of the marriage" while having affairs on the side, as a test. He believes that men need tests. I would agree. We all need tests to judge our own mettle. But similarly, a bank robber takes pride in his ability to rob banks and pickpockets take great pride in the skill and thrill of slipping a wallet out of a live man's pocket and walking away without notice. I would argue that the better test is making the marriage work, staying faithful through trials, overcoming problems. Is this not a better test? A test you might feel proud of?"

"Yes, I know, there are plenty of men who pass that test of

fidelity. For them there is no other way. Understand that an affair—an act that throws the ordinary into a direct balance with the extraordinary—is a kind of test, too. For me, it tests limits and my tolerance for risk. It does not simply feel good. It creates strata of secrecy that demand my constant upkeep. It requires attention to two sets of details—one for home and one for the hotel room— while managing huge swaths of attendant risk involving communication and implication. My stories must mesh. My memories must be private." Again, he is taking great pride in the same kind of deception that murder or thievery take. Yeah, it's a thrill but you can also take up skydiving where you will hurt no one but yourself.

"She tells me not to cheat on her. But I do, and I do not let her in

on it. I've fucked lesbians in Paris, hotel clerks on cots, and soldiers in uniform. All while I was married. I wish the list were longer. Sometimes it is banal, other times epic." This is kind of a "notches on your bedpost" type of pride, collecting/breaking hearts as a form of self-gratification and arrogance.

"Women will never understand how men can cheat because

they think of it in terms of themselves—as something done to them. They treat it as an affront first, as a breakdown in social order, then a wound, then a mortal wound. And this is a key. They do this because women are singular, in both their desire and their demands. This is why I serve women well. I treat them as planetary objects…." I can't help but think that if this man were cheated on by his wife (which he believes would never happen) that he would feel that it was 'something done to him' and that that something were certainly be an affront, a breakdown in social order and a wound.

"There is some thrill in it to be sure. Because more than anything,
cheating is a chance for the body to assert its dominion over the soul, to urge the individual toward his genetic rootspring, toward what feels good rather than what feels compulsory." Body over soul again- does he feels that the body should assert dominion over the soul. So what then is the value of his soul?

"She pulled me into her chest and whispered into my ear, "I love
you." I hushed her and said not to say that. "I know," she murmured, "but I do. I never respond to that. And I guess I got quiet then, because she threw the wrapper into a bowl of room-service cocktail sauce and asked me, a little coldly, "What should I say, then?"
I shrugged and lay down next to her. "Say what I always say," I
told her. She eased in against my hips and asked, "What's that?"
"Then I gave her my reason, my three magic words. "I need you[13]."
So, when a man tells you he needs you, he may mean he needs to *use* you.

There you have it: that's it. One man's description of what the reward is for him. The cheating is thrills, ego and hubris. Being able to deceive the person you are most intimate with is an accomplishment. It's cold, remorseless and utterly selfish.

Why a Man (or Woman) Might Not Cheat

"Infidelity is morally wrong…it shows that a man or woman has a character flaw or is immature…not an adult." John M., businessman

Steve Harvey, author of the best seller *Act Like a Lady, Think Like a Man*, says that men need three things: Your support (respect), loyalty and sex.[14] However, cheating is not to be allowed. He writes, "Women can go over and over everything in their minds finding all kinds of deficiencies in themselves—I didn't do this right, I wasn't good enough, I didn't love him the way I should…she came in here and outperformed me…but the fact remains that he had no business cheating."[15]

Steve's reasons are right to the point.

Men cheat because:
1)   They can. Men and women are different. Men can and do want to have sexual experiences without emotional connection. They crave sexual variety. They are biologically programmed to spread their offspring, while women are programmed to nest.
2)   They think they can get away with it.
3)   He has not become who he wants and needs to be or found who he truly wants.
4)   What's happening at home isn't happening the way it used to.
5)   The biggest reason of all: there's always a woman out there willing to cheat with him. [16]

"If he breaks his promise and steps out of the union anyway, you've got to be prepared to let him go and walk away. You can't find out he cheated, confront him and stay with him only to question his every move and nag him about what he is doing…Now sometimes it takes a man to lose something or nearly lose something to really appreciate it."

I once spoke with a husband and wife team of family educators and consultants. For 35 years, this very successful pair has worked together; saving marriages and helping people recover from unions that could not be saved. I asked the husband about infidelity.

"Is it true that most men would like to cheat?" He said, "Well I think that's probably true."

I asked "Would you?" He replied, "Uh, yes…I would like to have other relationships, if it were alright with my wife."

His wife's jaw dropped and she stared at him as though he had confessed to murder. Seeing her response, he quickly added, "Yeah, but I would never do that because I know I would lose her and I would never, ever risk what we have."

So, a man or woman might not cheat if they highly valued the relationship and knew the relationship would end. From this I would draw the conclusion that it's wise to let your spouse know up front that you would leave if he cheats—if this is what you would do.

Another reason not to cheat is commitment. You made a commitment. You made a promise; you are the kind of person who honors his commitments. You value your word, your honesty. When famous banker J.P. Morgan was asked how he decided who to lend money to, he said, "It's not about assets, it's about character." You look for character in the borrower as a more significant indication of repayment of debts. The same goes with marriage. What is your spouse's character?

Thoughts from Men Who Don't Cheat

It is estimated that 50 percent of men will cheat on a spouse, but that still leaves 50 percent who won't cheat.

Psychologist Bill R. said, "I feel that 'character' or the lack thereof, leads to cheating rather than being the inevitable product of an unhappy marriage. I used to say that any 'justification' for cheating is more appropriately a justification for divorce. Cheating is hypocritical and a violation of the Golden Rule which undergirds all morality. Character, integrity, morality are all essentially the same. Temptation can be understood, but cheating never."

Lee M., an elementary school teacher said, "Infidelity destroys one's character. Though the act itself is not necessarily an indication of who the participants truly are, they are never able to fully restore the trust, integrity, and sincerity that they had. It can never be reversed."

Page H., author of *Thin Places*, writes, "A powerful, dynamic, loving relationship and the act of cheating are incompatible actions, like faith and fear. The two can never coexist at the same time. Most mature relationships intrinsically know this and never practice alternatives."

And, so you don't think that all powerful men are cheaters, here are a few famous men who have shared why they chose not to cheat.

Billy Graham, when asked how he handled being on the road so much and being idolized by thousands of women said he made it his business to avoid any situation that might be tempting or even appear inappropriate. If he were going to meet a woman, any woman, whether it be a member of his congregation or a newswoman interviewing him or even a female head of state he would always have another member of his staff present. He indicated in interviews that he put time, effort and thought into avoiding difficult situations.

Jimmy Carter, famous for his "lusting in my heart" statement, never broke his vows. His strong commitment to his own values, as seen in his book on America's values, is the compass that keeps him faithful.

Warren Buffet, one of the world's most wealthy, powerful and influential movers and shakers, with every opportunity to cheat, is renowned for his attention to spouse and family.

So, you see, it is possible to be faithful, even if you are powerful and wealthy.

Who is most Likely to Cheat?

I don't want to say there is never a situation in which a person being unfaithful is justified. Human situations and relationships can be complex. People stay in bad marriages sometimes for good reasons. But cheaters who cheat for simple gratification, boredom, ego building or just lust are people without character. People without character have no moral boundaries to hold them in. Their word is not important to them.

Lying and cheating in other venues besides romance are a great clue that a person will have no compunctions in lying to you or cheating on you. It is always a mistake to think that a person's love for you will change them or at least protect you, the beloved, from the things they do to others.

If you look at the patterns of Jessie James, Tiger Woods, Bill Clinton and David Duchovney, to name just a few, infidelity seems to be serial in nature. Once a man or woman strays, it seems they are compelled to repeat the pattern again and again. It is an essentially selfish act, one that risks the heart of the person who loves them, and the hearts of their children. It is an activity that weakens the fabric of marriages, families and perhaps worst of all minimizes the value of trust in relationships between individuals.

Aside than character, there are also qualities that tend to occur frequently in cheaters. A Web site called *The Truth about Deception*[17] lists these: he or she would likely be more attractive than average, someone who travels a lot, has the opportunity to meet people, tends to be self-centered, has power and/or money, charisma, has a strong sex drive, a sense of entitlement due to their status and power; and if they are having relational problems, feel neglected or underappreciated.

Preventing Cheating

In the end, the why doesn't really matter. What matters is that the person you have entrusted your heart to is capable of crossing the line and is capable of doing it again. You may decide to stay with him or her but you know you cannot really trust them completely again. The only way to prevent cheating is to marry a man or woman whose innate character believes in commitment and rejects cheating and lying.

Dr. Joyce Hudson is an Assistant Clinical Professor of Psychiatry at the Virginia Commonwealth University School of Medicine, a Licensed Clinical Psychologist and she carries a certified AASECT diploma in sex therapy. She has 30 years of experience as a marriage counselor, and has dealt with a wide variety of relationship issues including sexual problems.[18] She has counseled more than 1,800 couples.

She did her pre- and post-doctorate work at what was then the Family Living Program at the Virginia Commonwealth University School of Medicine, Department of Psychiatry. After working with numerous couples there, she decided that if clients saw the potential difficulties in their relationships, they could make better choices in partners and avoid serious problems later.

She took a two-year sabbatical to develop a pre-marital counseling program. She discovered though, that most couples she worked with who had concerns about their compatibility, found being "in love" just too appealing to let logic define their path. She says, "Love overcame reason every time." Of the couples she advised against marriage, almost all went ahead with their plans and a year or more later, came back to her saying, "I wish I had listened to you."

Her work is now geared to making existing relationships work better. She says, "Marriage therapy can help, but if couples wait too long, they have a closetful of painful and difficult experiences to go through." Then it's a question of believing the same things will not happen again and forgiving.

"The capacity to forgive is key." She believes that to choose a good partner, one needs to know the character of the individual. She believes that character is developed in childhood and rarely changes after that. Her theory is that "the person we marry is their character."

An exception to this is if a person makes a mistake that is totally out of his usual, historical character and takes responsibility, apologizes and feels sincere remorse about what he has done. That may mean it won't happen again. Infidelity can be one of those mistakes. Is your sex life an excuse to cheat? She has seen couples where there are no sexual problems but one partner cheats. And others where there might be no sex at all, but neither spouse would ever consider cheating. So, no excuses there.

She adds, "If I stand up there and say till death do us part...I am saying you can trust me. I give you my faith, you make a commitment. Marriage takes work and commitment. A true commitment is like putting a date in your planner in ink, not pencil." [19]

Part III
Is This Happening to You?

Chapter 8
What to Do about It

"When your lover is a liar, you and he have a lot in common; you're both lying to you." Susan Forward

If you find yourself in this situation, the thought that your spouse may be cheating on you is so emotionally overwhelming that you have an urgent need to know at all costs. If you ask them whether they are cheating, innocent or not, they will deny all. Or, they may admit it and you may not be prepared to respond. In either case, you may have put them on notice that you know. Do not confront them at this point, even though you are dying to. Wait until you have more information and a sense of how you really want to handle this.

Becoming a Detective

Private investigators say that Valentine's Day is one of their busiest days of the year.

That's the day that cheating men (and women) visit their honeys with romantic gifts and liaisons. It's the perfect day to catch them. (Christmas is another prime time.) If you want to know what is going on there are numerous options these days.

You can hire a detective. They are expensive but will allow you to be hands-off. Cindy Patterson, private investigator, says it takes two things to prove infidelity. The first is opportunity for a sexual liaison (as in leaving a hotel or house) and the second is demonstrated affection (as in a kiss on the cheek.) So the movie stereotype of the video of the cheaters caught "in flagrante' delicato" is not necessary.

Cindy agrees that once your suspicions are confirmed you must not tell your spouse what you know and how you know. She said, "Most off the time, my clients want to stop the cheating spouse by telling them what they know. That seldom works. If you share with the spouse that you hired a detective, you have blown any future chance of checking on them."

She wants you to know that your spouse is now your enemy. She recommends keeping all information to yourself—let them think you are oblivious. "If you must tell them, you can say, 'I know you are having an affair,' but not tell them how you know."

A less expensive option is to trail your spouse yourself, taking photos, collecting emails, and gathering computer data and credit card records (that may show gifts or liaisons.) You need documentation that shows a connection or trail.

In Ivana Trump's book *The Best is Yet to Come,*[20] she quotes famed New York divorce attorney Raoul Felder, as saying, "Look at credit cards to see a pattern—lunch for one, then lunch for two—charges for gifts close to the holidays that you can't account for."

Get close to his secretary if he has one and if it is feasible, as she will likely know what is happening. (Unless, of course, you think she is the one.) My husband's secretary knew everything but did not tell me because she did not want to hurt me. I wish she had. Former secretaries can also be very helpful in getting you the information you need.

The downside of becoming your own detective is that spying on someone you have a close relationship with will make you feel weird. Get over it. Your emotional life is at stake. You would not be doing this without reason and this person may no longer be your best friend.

There are an enormous number of technological gadgets that can get you the info you need. Simple things like baby monitors can be used to listen in on activity. If it is your phone, you can attach a recorder. Global positioning devices can be attached to your partner's car, which can give you a record of where your spouse goes and who he sees. Cameras can be small enough to be hidden anywhere, even in clocks or air purifiers.

There are programs you can download onto your spouse's laptop that enable you to view his email messages. There is also a keyboard log stroke decoder, a one-inch cable that fits onto the computer and registers every keystroke. It can spit out a document that shows every email, every web site and password your spouse has been typing. It is legal if used on your home (co-owned) computer. There is even, unbelievably, a semen detector that uses infrared light to show semen stains in cars, on sofas, on sheets. Just Google the phrases "Catch a Cheat" or "Cheating Spouse" and you will find more information than you need.

The most important thing, according to private Investigator Patterson, is that you realize this person can no longer be trusted. She said, "I never accept a case where my client is emotionally ambivalent. There is no point, they will tell the spouse everything. Then the spouse hides all future activity."

She adds that cheating is usually a pattern. "If you tell your spouse you know, they may be so sorry—'I'll quit, it's over, I'm sorry—but then he will go back to that person." This is a game, and you must play to win.

The Value of Proving Adultery

Proving adultery in court may or may not be important. In some courts, with some judges, it may affect their decisions regarding settlement, child visitation and alimony. More importantly, It may give you leverage with your soon to be ex. Most valuable of all however, it may give you the certainty you need to choose your life's direction.

Dan Butler, an attorney specializing in family law in Richmond, Va., says proving adultery may affect alimony determination. Some judges will give favored treatment to a spurned wife. Also, the new girlfriend may not want her affair with your spouse publicized, particularly if she is married. In this case, the fear of discovery may be the thing that gives you leverage with your spouse. Conversely, if your spouse can turn the table and prove you have been unfaithful, you may forfeit alimony. (So be very careful of having relationships that can trip you up prior to finalizing your divorce.)

It may be important to the court to show that your spouse used family money to enhance his love life. With custody, you can insist through the court that your spouse not have a person of the opposite sex in the house during child visitation. Even though it may not be important in court, your spouse's fidelity is still the most important question you need answered for your own sanity.

Financial Steps to Take Now

"The better part of valor is discretion, in the which better part I have saved my life," William Shakespeare

Stacy Schneider[21], suggests that before you confront your spouse, do the following:

1) Establish your own bank account. You can legally take one-half of your cash and put it in your own account. Bear in mind this may tip your hand.
2) Get your own credit card in your own name—while still married.

3)   Establish credit by taking out a loan in your name and paying it off right away.

4)   Stay in the family home while the divorce is underway. If your husband stops paying you can ask the court to intervene. You would get a lawyer to file the motion. If he claims he has no money—he can get out of it—you keep paying the payments to hold the house from foreclosure.

5)   Start a cash reserve fund for yourself—pocket your pay and any extra money. Sell things you own yourself. If you're pocketing your own pay, he may later try to claim a portion through community property laws in states such as California, Nevada, Idaho, Louisiana, Texas, Arizona, Mexico, Washington and Wisconsin.

6)   Open your own safe deposit box for papers and valuables.

7)   You may want to get your own P.O. Box, computer and a new, private email account.

Documents you need copies of include financial records, copies of all life insurance policies, CDs, car titles, annuities, bank accounts, deeds, retirement benefits, certificates of ownership for valuables, wills and trusts (these often show property), tax returns, pay stubs, inventory of property with value of same, loan statements, bills that show value of purchased automobiles, furnishings, other expensive items, a copy of his credit report, charge card records and bills (can show signs of an affair.)

If these are too difficult to obtain and you feel there are hidden assets, forensic accountants can be hired to find hidden assets and money. You have the right to freeze all joint accounts but let him know you have done that. Do not overspend or steal; it will hurt you ultimately in court.

Stacy added that if, it is at all possible, keep it amicable. Expressing your feelings may give you a lift temporarily, but may make a settlement much more difficult to reach. In any negotiation there are the tangibles of the deal: money, assets, real estate, alimony, and support. However, there are also elements of emotion such as the need to win, the need to feel fairly treated, and the desire for revenge. Do not let your emotional needs hurt your chances of getting a desirable settlement.

Raoul Felder, the previously mentioned divorce attorney[22], said, "Every man of wealth has a piece of paper somewhere that has his net worth on it, every penny."

It will be far easier for you to get information about financial assets before your spouse becomes aware that you know he is cheating. Once the cat is out of the bag, your spouse may take whatever he can get, hide some more and get out of town. If he goes out of state or hides assets, you will have a difficult time trying to get them back. Remember, possession is nine-tenths of the law. Not to say that you should seize everything, but try to gain control of at least half and document the existence of anything else.

One thing I did not know—and that cost me a bundle—is that if you inherited money during your marriage that money does not have to be split with your spouse even if you have co-mingled the funds. So keep records of any money you may have inherited.

Another thing to consider is taxes. In my situation, I had paid the year's estimated taxes out of joint funds before I realized my marriage was in trouble. After we split, I filed separately and asked for 50 percent of those payments to be attributed to my tax liability for that year. However, my husband claimed all of them on his return. Tax law says that if a couple disagrees on this issue, the person with the biggest tax bill gets a higher percentage of the credit. His income was high, mine was negligible, so he got the tax credits. Had I known that would happen, I would have not made any estimated payments.

Chapter 9
Is It Over?

"Ever has it been that love knows not its own depth until the hour of separation." Kahlil Gibran

On my 60th birthday my husband left to meet Melissa at a conference where he listed her as his partner. It was a conference I was also registered for. We had gone to it together every year for 15 years. Her husband would be there too. I would be allowed to go if I did not tell her husband about the affair. I did not go.

Later, my husband told me he met the man, shook his hand and received the man's thanks for helping his wife with her business career. I said, "So you shook this guy's hand, the one who has leukemia, you shook his hand, accepted his thanks and made like you were his good friend? Is that right, while you were fucking his wife, yes?"

Then he came home again. He made intense, passionate love to me every chance he got. I let him, I loved him and wanted him and thought that meant he still loved me and that somehow we could work things out. It didn't mean that at all. The emotional turmoil we were in intensified our chemistry, or perhaps he merely figured it was his last opportunity to have sex with me. Throwing me a bone, he said I was a much better lover than Melissa.

There was a summer family reunion scheduled for an island off the coast of Florida. It was a tradition extending back to the first year of our marriage. Condo and air reservations had been in place long before I learned about his affair. One of my sons was coming from California. My other son was coming with his wife and two children from Colorado. They had grown up with Rob and loved him. His niece, Sue was coming from Philadelphia. Other people too. We all looked forward to this. No one knew about the affair. I wanted to have this one last time together with my family. It would be the last time. I foolishly hoped it would be a good memory for us all.

But Melissa called constantly. She must have known he had some ambivalence, and she did not want to lose the struggle for his affections. He took every call. At first, he left the room or turned away. But then, he just spoke to her in front of me as though it were all perfectly acceptable. He was planning a "business" trip to Costa Rica with her. He asked me for some of my air points so she could be in first class with him. I could not believe it. He said, "Surely you understand that we would want to be together?"

I asked him to get off the phone, to stop talking. He kept talking to her. Something inside of me snapped. I pulled the blue tooth off his ear and threw it. He grabbed the cell and started to talk again. I began to hit him with my fists. All my pain came pouring out. I was completely out of control.

We were on a screened porch. He went down on the ground and I continued to strike him. A man outside seeing this said, "Stop it lady, you are killing him. I'm calling the police." That brought me out of it. I could have killed him. Had I something close at hand, I might have. Appalled at what I had done. I said, "You will have to leave." I left then and went to my son's condo. My husband did leave and asked my son to drive him to the airport.

Can the Marriage Survive?

Hopefully, at this point, you have taken steps to protect yourself and your children legally and financially. You have spoken with an attorney whose advice you trust and now you know your options.

Armed with those options, legal advice, knowledge of assets and, we hope, some funds, you can either pretend you do not know or confront him. This is a tough decision, particularly if you have children. You have to consider if your marriage can be saved after this kind of exposure.

If infidelity happens, can the marriage survive? Dr. Hudson recommends you examine these questions: "How much lying was involved? How much cheating and for how long? Was abandonment of spouse and/or child involved? It's not just the cheating it's also the lying. Culture molds codes of honor. What is your code of honor? What is your lover's? It can work only if there are no excuses, no blaming and if the unfaithful partner takes full responsibility."

Who knows? What you do know now is that your spouse can lie to you, can cheat on you and was willing to risk the entire relationship with you and possibly risk his children. This bit of information will forever change your view of him, the value of the marriage to you and your future piece of mind. You can never fully trust this person again and if you choose to stay with him, you will have to be vigilant forever. That does not mean the marriage cannot continue—there are plenty of high-profile men who have cheated and gone on with their marriages—but it does mean that everything has changed.

Psychologists say that behavior patterns that are established tend to change only when significant trauma occurs. Bill Rhodes, a psychologist with more than 30 years experience in counseling said on this point: "Yes, I think cheaters can and do change but I want to know what the turning point was for them in their life that led them to abandon that way of 'being in the world.' This is the same for alcoholics who stop drinking. I want to know about what happened (did they hit bottom?) to give up that way of life. I won't accept vague stuff like, 'I just outgrew it' or 'I got tired of it.' I want to hear that they 'lost everything I loved because of booze and learned to live a completely different life,' etc. I want to hear him talk about the pain he caused himself and others, how he could no longer respect himself, how lost the best relationship in his life for a fling, whatever. An unacceptable answer would be, 'I stopped cheating when I met you 'cause you are all I need'."

The Dangers of Denial

Mary Jo Buttafuoco, wife of the notorious Joey Buttafuoco, believed him when he said he was completely innocent of having an affair even after his 16-year-old girlfriend shot Mary Jo in the head. She still believed him after he pled guilty to statutory rape (he said he did not have relations with the girl but that he would be convicted anyway.) It was not until he was arrested for soliciting a hooker that she finally realized what a total animal she was married to.

As events happened in the marriage, Joey Buttafuoco came up with excuse after incredible excuse. In her book, *Getting it through my Thick Skull*[23], she explains how her love for him clouded truths that seemed so very obvious to the rest of the world. If your spouse has a history of "mistakes" it is likely that he will continue with this behavior.

Cindy, the detective, said that in her experience most cheating spouses, after a brief time of penitence, go back to their flame on the side. David Hulbert and Sherry Finneran of the Family Education Center in Richmond, Va., say it is possible but difficult to repair the damage of an affair. They say the cheating spouse must in every way make his spouse aware of all that is going on in his life. No emotional relationships with members of the opposite sex. No secrets, no hidden passwords on computers, no hidden codes on telephone message machines.

One problem with acceptance is that the cheater may feel he got away with it once so he can again. There have to be some kind of ramifications and a check-and-balance system. Where are we now? Are there signs? Are we close emotionally right now?

On the other hand, Cindy said, "If you do take the person back and 'forgive' them you can't keep pointing the finger and throw it in their face. That won't work." You should perhaps forgive but not forget! Don't be a bitch or an ogre or weepy. Act in control and calm. Do not relieve them of their guilt by being an ass. "You have some power as the offended party, but if you want the marriage, don't keep throwing it in their face and don't tell others about how badly you have been treated."

Steve Harvey, in his book *Act Like a Lady, Think Like a Man*, writes that he believes it's possible to repair a marriage with a terrible breach of trust; possible but very difficult. As he says, "If you go forward with a man once he cheats you must demand complete honesty from your spouse, stay close and be ready to leave if he transgresses."

In deciding whether or not to leave a marriage, your family and friends can be either a great source of support or your worst advisors. They may be fearful of how you will survive alone. A friend's mother said to her, "But, you are so argumentative and such a bad housekeeper, you'll never find another husband." She stayed in a miserable marriage way too long, wasted many years and ultimately left anyway.

Another friend from a very traditional culture was set up by her family in an arranged marriage. It turned out that her husband was gay and did not want sex, nor children, nor did he give her any attention and he treated her as a servant. She lost eight years to her family's injunction that she must stay married. After finally leaving, while she incurred her families anger, she found a wonderful man who was totally devoted to her.

So, if your marriage is miserable anyway, you should get out as fast as you can with no backward glance. If it's been a good marriage, you might want to assess if it is salvageable.

There are Options

You may not realize it but you do have options. You may feel if your spouse has cheated that you must end the marriage. Or, you may feel that no matter what they have done, for religious or traditional reasons that you are supposed to stay in the marriage. You may feel you do not have the finances to separate, especially if you are not working or have children. But, the reality is, you can choose your path.

Open your mind and think creatively. If you have not confronted your spouse, you have time to plan. Think about the timing of the separation: Is your husband due a bonus or other windfall in the near future? Don't separate until after it arrives, so it will be community property. Think about Social Security: If you've been married nine years, you might want to stick out the last year so you can collect on your ex's earnings record. By the way, if you separate but stay married, most states will give you one third or more of your husband's estate if he dies before you. This holds true even if he has written you out of his will. So you might consider splitting but staying married. Remember though, that if you die first, he has the same right to go after a portion of your estate.

Finally, don't just pack your bags, load up the kids, and drive away in a car that needs four new tires. Before you separate, perform maintenance on the car. Get yourself a new wardrobe and whatever other tools you may need for your new life. You might decide, as one woman did, to stay, but with a five year plan. She knew her husband was cheating. She did not confront him. Instead she enrolled in a college course that would help her increase her income. She set as her goals: additional education, an increased amount of savings in her own private bank account and a wider set of social connections. She gave herself a five-year timeline and wrote down what she needed to accomplish it. Only then would she make her break, when she was financially and socially in a better place.

Mary Jo Buttafuoco, after finally coming to the realization that she was married to a sociopath, set herself up in a separate apartment, paid for and furnished by her husband, who was trying to get her back, and enrolled in college courses so she could create a career and financial independence for herself.

If You Want Him to Stay

As Cindy Patterson remarks, men indeed are more practical in their view of love, romance and marriage. My husband asked at one point, if he came back would he get one-half of our assets back? I was so astonished I just looked at him, as if he were someone brand new in my life. He could not possibly be the man I had spent the last 20 years with. I also remember him saying that he considered staying but that I would keep him on a "short leash" and that he would not be able to stand that. This was a decision of logic not heart.

It brought back a memory of his single friend, Charles, in the midst of a two-year intense love affair with a single mom. He had moved into her life, her heart and her home, bonding with her daughter in the role of step-dad. It looked like they were headed for marriage.

But then, he decided it was important for his career to get another degree (he already had one master's) and that the best place would be an out-of-state university that would necessitate a move for about three years, maybe more. He was leaving. She could not go with him as her job was local. She had a child to support. He was not going to even ask her. He felt it would be best for him to find someone else as he did not want the "inconvenience" of a long-distance relationship.

My husband and I both pointed out to him (practically pleading) that he had several fine universities in our city to choose from. He did not have to move. How could he leave his lover and her child when he loved them and they loved him so?

His response was he was not going to let "a relationship" stand in the way of his getting the very best degree program he could. No emotion there, just a totally selfish perspective. He left them. The mother and daughter were devastated. We were devastated. It was painful to watch her grieve but more so to see her surprise. Yes, my husband agreed, Charles was a selfish prick.

In Louise DeSalvo's book *Adultery*, she described what happened when she found out her husband was having an affair. He was an intern in medical school involved with a nurse. The husband was talking about leaving her and their six-month-old baby. In a state of hysteria, she went to the crib, lifted up the screaming baby and, as she puts it, shoved the baby in his face, telling him he would have to take the child with him if he left. He said he did not believe she could part with the baby. She said, "try me."

Her mother advised her to go away with him for a few days and told her to "sleep with him, even if it makes you cry, sleep with him." Here the wise mom was telling her daughter to let him know that if he stays, sex will continue. He will not be beaten up every day. Her mom tells her to be calm, an oasis of calm, in what for the husband at this moment be must be a maelstrom world. He assesses his situation: go with his gorgeous blond mistress, bringing screaming young infant with him or stay with wife who will be calm, take care of said infant and continue to provide him with sex. He decides to stay. So there you have it: putting practicality and ease onto the decision-making scales of the male mind.

Now, it is also true that many men, as I have pointed out, will risk throwing it all away, many times over. And each time they get away with it, it reinforces their belief that they are beyond disaster. They keep it up until it is a disaster and they do lose it all. As did Tiger Woods until he lost his wife, children and millions in endorsement dollars.

But if faced with the truth of a situation in which what they have (nonnagging wife, good sex, all their assets, no alimony or child support) is better than what they want (sexy mistress, custody and care of children, loss of social respect, loss of assets), their tendency will be to err on the side of keeping their assets, their name and their life but only when it is very real and right in front of their face.

If you stay, and if he stays, the one thing you have now that you did not have before is knowledge of the way things really are. And, as Louise de Salvo and Julie Metz both say, that knowledge is freeing. No more living for the other—more living for self and the children.

If You Decide to Stay

If you decide to stay, one way you can take a chance with your old spouse again is to have him put his money where his mouth is. Have him sign an agreement saying that if he cheats (you must define cheat and what would be considered proof of that) you get everything.

If he is ready, willing and able to sign that…at least it shows he believes he can be faithful. If he cannot sign that, what is he willing to bet on his own pledge to be faithful? If it's not a lot then he has little confidence in himself or his promises. In the state of Virginia, signs of affection (i.e. kiss in public) and opportunity (i.e. an evening at her house) are what is required as proof of infidelity. Make sure a lawyer agrees that this will hold up in court. This is not such a bad idea going into your next marriage and can be included in the form of a pre-nuptial.

Accepting Reality

The most mentally healthy thing you can do is arrive at acceptance of the realities of the situation as soon as you are able. In the novel *First Wives Club*, Annie, the main character, is walking through the zoo. She muses on the wisdom of letting her ex back into her life.

"For a moment she felt sorry for her ex-husband Aaron. But Aaron does not love me, she thought. He's just like those bears. They don't look dangerous but they are. Let a wild beast back into your life, the moment he does not get what he wanted from you, the moment he no longer needed her nurturing or felt deprived of it, he would attack and destroy her. Or leave her as he had already done…"[19]

Part IV
Everything You Need to Know About Divorce

Chapter 10
It's Over and You Want Out

"*Divorce is the psychological equivalent of a triple coronary bypass.*" Mary Kay Blakely

Finding a Lawyer

Your lawyer will be one of the most expensive investments you make, not only from the standpoint of fees but also in relation to your family's financial destiny and peace of mind—so finding a quality lawyer is critical. He or she should be experienced in this type of law, respected by peers and have references that will tell you he is responsive, creative, supportive and collaborative. His objective should be to help you achieve your goals. He should want to help you work things out without going to court, if possible.

Andrea Stiles, the family law attorney, recommends that when trying to find a good lawyer, you should "first of all, talk to people. Have they worked with an attorney they can recommend? Remember too, that two people can have differing opinions of the same lawyer."

She suggests looking in the *Martindale Hubble Guide*, a lawyer referral guide that rates lawyers on a peer review basis. Use only those rated "A" or "B." You may also consult the *American Academy of Matrimonial Lawyers Directory*. Inclusion in this book is based on very high standards, written and oral exams, and recommendations.

Next, interview three lawyers. A one-hour consult is worth every penny and may be the best investment you can make. Bring a tape recorder or a friend. You may be too upset to remember everything the attorney says. Ask the attorney whether he or an associate will represent you. How fast does he return calls? Does he seem tired or jaded? Is he listening? What is his schedule like? His billing practices? His view of litigation versus settlement?

Many people think they want a "pit bull" type of lawyer. Andrea warns against this. "You don't want one of these guys. They do not think, they use no strategy, they just attack. They ruin any chance of collaboration. Look for smart, competent and energetic representation. They look out for your best interest in the long term, not the pit bull. Pit bulls only cost you money." Andrea also recommends newer forms of divorce such as collaborative divorce, described below, as a cost- and emotion-saving alternative to traditional divorce.

Forms of Divorce
"A lawyer is never entirely comfortable with a friendly divorce, anymore than a good mortician wants to finish his job and then have the patient sit up on the table." Jean Kerr

In a traditional divorce, the husband and wife are each represented by their own attorneys in an antagonistic conflict. However, there are other methods of handling a divorce and these methods can be much more civilized and far less expensive. They include mediation and collaborative divorce.

A bright spot in the arena of divorce is the collaborative divorce process. Unlike mediation, which is binding in court, all information shared in the collaborative process cannot be used later in a courtroom if the negotiations fail. This allows parties to speak freely and be honest.

While most divorce settlements where a clear fifty-fifty split of assets is typical, the collaborative method takes a creative approach to a settlement. It is geared toward finding and meeting the most important needs of all parties involved and bringing the situation to a win-win conclusion. While mediation can be adversarial, collaborative divorce is neutral. It is not legal advice, but simply a process of coming up with a settlement that meets both parties' needs as much as possible. You will still need a lawyer for collaborative divorce.

Ms. Stiles said, "What I like about this process is it is non-adversarial. It is a team model. If parties cannot come to terms using this collaborative process then they must resort to starting again with a new attorney. It is an interest-based negotiation. It's about what is most important to you in this settlement, not just money. It can include a team of therapists, attorneys and experts working together. What is agreed upon in this process does not become legally binding until put into a legal document."

In discussing collaboration, Andrea gave two examples of how attorneys in a collaborative divorce can meet the real needs of both parties through creative thinking. In one case, a woman with two children, who had been in a long-term marriage, was being divorced. Her husband's family was wealthy and had a trust set up that owned the house they lived in. The family wanted the children to be able to stay in the same school district and neighborhood. The mother, who had not worked outside the home for years, wanted to stay at home until the children were old enough to attend school. She did not have the money to pay the mortgage. Her husband's family also wanted to make sure that their son still had a house to live in, yet all parties agreed the couple could not stay in the same house.

The attorneys suggested that the trust sell the large house the couple lived in and purchase two smaller ones in the same neighborhood. The big house was sold by the trust, and the money went back into the trust, which then bought two smaller homes. One was rented by the wife for a nominal amount. The husband moved into the other house. The husband, the wife and the trust were all satisfied by this solution; one that never would have occurred through a traditional divorce process.

In another case, a 65-year-old woman with health issues had been receiving support from her ex-husband for years. The ex-husband, now 71 years old, wanted to retire and end the support. The wife was afraid she would wind up destitute and on the street. They were ready to go to court. Instead, using the collaborative process, they located an assisted living facility that will take care of her for life and provide for all her needs for one lump sum. The wife was satisfied. The husband agreed to this one-time payment as it freed him from all future obligations. Again, a win-win for both parties was achieved.

Mediation is another way to try to resolve disputes prior to going to court. As does collaborative divorce, mediation helps avoid costly litigation fees and reduces conflict between parties. Richmond, VA., attorney Dan Butler says, "In mediation, a person is appointed to guide you and your spouse through the process. You agree upfront that the mediator's judgment will be accepted. The outcome is legally binding." He estimates that mediation is successful 90 percent of the time, which is a higher percentage of success than reached with collaboration.

Money and Assets

Today, assets, including cash from the sale of a home, are commonly split in half. But there are many exceptions to that. If a pre-nuptial exists, if one partner is substantially more wealthy than the other, if one of the spouses is handicapped or ill, if there are children involved, if one person has deliberately hidden, stolen or squandered family assets and that can be proved—all these things can affect a settlement.

If you follow Stacy Schneider's suggestions (printed a few pages back) on getting your finances in order before filing for divorce, you should have most of the information you need to determine family assets and income.

In my case, inherited monies made up a large portion of our savings. I had inheritance from several relatives and put those funds into joint accounts with my husband. I split all of this with him fifty-fifty. I later learned from another attorney that inherited monies, even if co-mingled, are still the property of the person who inherits. Your attorney can explain to you what your state courts typically approve.

Also, when my husband and I discussed separation, my intention was to split everything with him fifty-fifty. But, as it dawned on me that I would have no income, I became angry and a better advocate for myself.

Before we were married, I had worked as a marketing specialist for a hospital; a job I really enjoyed. After we were married, my husband wanted to start his own business and asked me to work with him. My initial marketing work landed him his biggest client, one that continued producing a stream of other clients and was the foundation of the business. While my husband's talent and genius as a business consultant was the product, my time and energy helped shape the business especially initially.

By the time he met Melissa, he and I had been in business together for 20 years. While working in the business I took courses towards a master's degree with the idea I would go back to work in marketing. But after I got the degree, he said he needed me to continue working with him and not leave the business. As many women do, I was living with the delusion that I had emotional and financial security.

By a fluke, I got to keep the house. When we were married, we bought our house together, putting equal amounts down. But, because I was concerned about his ambivalence toward monogamy, I had him sign a pre-nuptial saying it would be mine should we break up. I forgot about this paper and found it by accident while going through the safety deposit box. When I showed it to him, my husband was furious. I was so relieved. If I had had to go out and find a new place to live at that time I think I would have had a mental breakdown.

Remember that for your next marriage: pre-nuptials are good things. I share all this with you because you may be so hurt and overwrought that you just want to give in and be done with it. But you cannot do that, especially if you have children.

Property
In deciding about who gets property, keep in mind your most important objectives. Do not get into a battle for control, let small things go. Try to make this a win-win. Maintain as much good will as possible between you

and your spouse. Give up things that are not going to be important in the long run. Many couples lose all perspective and argue over ridiculous items when they can trade relatively unimportant items for the elements that are most important to them.

Custody

Everything done regarding custody should be in the best interest of the children. Allow them to continue to care about your spouse. Do not make things more difficult for them in an effort to hurt your ex. (See Chapter 12 on Helping Your Children Get Through a Divorce.) If there is another woman involved, do not make her your enemy. She may be caring for your children at times and it will be in your interest to be able to communicate with her.

If you think your spouse may try to gain full custody of the children, then you must be prepared to fight. Be careful to be above reproach in your own behavior. Do not leave your children with a boyfriend if you have one and do not have a boyfriend in the house overnight when your children are in your house. Do not leave your children unattended. If your spouse has a history of bad behavior with the children keep a journal of those incidents, citing dates, times and witnesses.

Can't Afford a Divorce?

Lynn Melville is the author of several books and a blog on relationships, divorce and abuse. In particular, she focuses on the difficulties of marriage to individuals with borderline personality disorder. Below is a reprint of an essay by Jody Williams that appeared in Lynn Melville's blog, stoptheabuse.com, on the topic of how to obtain a divorce from a disturbed, abusive husband when you have no money.

How to Get a Divorce When You're Broke, an essay by Jody Williams

"My ex got me fired from my job, evicted from my apartment, and stole my car when I threw him out. Affording a lawyer was out of the question for me. If I hadn't been a paralegal, I NEVER would have been able to get myself through the legal maze I had to go through.

I found out that even most lawyers don't know or don't take the time to enforce garnishment of wages, tax returns, and paychecks and bank accounts for judgments, even though it's usually a simple matter of filling out forms.

Fees were a hard one for me. I learned that because I had to file for welfare (to feed myself and our baby to get away from him), I could get all the fees waived. I got the court fees for the filing of the divorce petition and the service from the marshal waived by showing them proof that I was on welfare.

Everyone in the United States is entitled to legal help, even if they can't afford it. Court fees and service fees of legal papers to the opposing party can be waived in any state if you can prove you're poor.

You don't have to be on welfare. You can show them a bank statement, an income statement or some notarized statement that you're broke. They have a separate form you fill out to have a judge approve the waiving of your court fees.

Lawyer's fees can't be waived—only court fees. Even copying fees for your papers can be waived once you have the form signed by a judge.

You don't even have to go to the hearing. You just mail in the appropriate forms to the court, the judge stamps it, and then you can show it to get all fees waived.

As for hidden bank accounts you don't know about, you can go to places like www.freecreditreport.com and order a credit report for free, since you know his information (social security number, address, etc.). Usually that site will show you any open accounts. It may not show all of them, but a lot of them will show up. You'd be surprised what you can find out about someone from a credit report. They pop it up online, and you can print it out right there—free.

If you don't know where they are working, usually even their job will show up on the credit report. From that information, you'll know where to go to garnish wages.

If they're expecting an income tax return, you can let the IRS know that you want to garnish that for payment of a judgment order from the court.

To find hidden bank accounts not showing up on the credit report (or that they might have joint with someone else as the main account holder), you can call any of the banks you think this person might have an account with. You probably know the full name, social security number and birth date of this person. With that information, you can call that bank and 'pretend' to be them and having lost your account number. They ask for birth date and social security number—and then will give you the account number.

To get contempt of an order of the court, the lawyers usually have to file for a hearing to have that done. Most lawyers don't like to do this—and then there's the problem of having no money to pay their fee. There are forms you can fill out to represent yourself and ask for this kind of hearing.

If you can't afford a lawyer, you can represent yourself. In every state I've lived in, this means you write in your name on the forms, then the words 'in pro per'. This means you're representing yourself. You also write in your contact information instead of a lawyer's contact information.

Very important, you are allowed to use a post office box if you don't want to give out your home address.

Every place I've lived in besides Las Vegas has forms you can fill out in pen for just about everything you need done. They also usually have some kind of family law help center where you can get free forms and advice. If you can't find one near you in the phone book (because they all have different names), you can call up your nearest law library and ask them where to find it. They'll know where it is.

As for garnishing wages or bank accounts or whatever, there are forms to get a judge to order that garnishment once you have a judgment. You have to file to get a garnishment order from the judge. Then a marshal or sheriff (whoever it is in your state that the courts use to serve their papers) will go to the employer or bank and attach the money—or take it and freeze it—or whatever is appropriate.

Almost all towns have a law library. You can ask the librarian for a book of court forms. They have copies of all of the forms available that you can just fill out yourself. All libraries and law libraries have books that are called Rules of Court—for your local courthouse. Those will tell you what papers are needed, how to file them, where and what the fees are, etc.

You can also look up a lot about statutes and laws in your town online. Some courthouses even have forms you can just download online. Not all courts, and not all the forms, are available online though. So visiting a law library or even the main or local library (if your town is too small), can help you. All libraries either have court or legal books—or they can refer you to the library that does.

I have sued people, defended myself, and collected judgments, handled two divorces and gotten child support orders. All kinds of stuff I've done myself for free—using the Internet, the law libraries and the family law centers when I needed help. And almost all of my suits and service fees I've gotten waived because I was broke.

You can also try Prepaid Legal. For $35 for a month of service, you can get lawyers to give you advice, review papers and even give you appropriate court forms and tell you where and how to file them. I've used them successfully on simple matters, when I've needed the intimidation of a lawyer to call or write a letter, help me with legal research or to get certain forms. They are cheaper than a lawyer in their own private practice.

But be warned—Prepaid legal attorneys are usually first-year lawyers and not the sharpest tool in the shed."

This is excellent information. It shows just how much you can accomplish on your own with courage, persistence and the right advice.

Chapter 11
I Go to a Lawyer

"A divorce is like an amputation: you survive it, but there's less of you."
Margaret Atwood

During this time, I sought the advice of an attorney a friend recommended. I made an appointment. When I went to his office, I had not slept for a week and had already lost five pounds. My heart beat was fast and irregular, and I looked like a wreck from sleeplessness and crying.

The receptionist looked at me in alarm, and ushered me into a conference room where I would not be out in public. She offered water and looked at me with concern. The room was an executive conference room; the kind with a huge, well-shined mahogany round table and padded leather swivel chairs, a place to do deals and conduct business.

I thoroughly embarrassed myself by not just tearing up, but sobbing off and on. The attorney, middle-aged, smooth and attractive, entered the room handed me Kleenex as necessary and waited patiently between crying jags for me to get my story out. I wanted some kind of document that would separate our assets so that aspect of the divorce would be finished before he left on another trip. Discussion and negotiation would be all the more difficult if done via long distance.

The attorney, with the cool air of detachment a surgeon might have, had me list the big assets from memory and told me to get together a more detailed list. We drew up a draft that split everything fifty-fifty. Included was money I had inherited from both of my parents and my uncle. As I mentioned before, I did not realize that inheritance does not have to be shared. Also, no suggestion was made by the attorney for alimony of any kind. I was too shell-shocked to think in those terms.

It was not until just before we were to sign these documents that I, realizing I was about to be in real financial distress, and thoroughly stung by Rob's obvious intention to cut me out of the business with no concern for where my future income might come from, requested a separate sum of money to serve as an alimony of sorts. I simply pulled a figure out of the air. I should have had an intelligent discussion with a financial planner or the attorney so that the alimony amount would actually relate to the income I had been living on while in the marriage. I also wanted to not have to chase him for monthly payments and thought that a lump sum would make things more agreeable. When I asked for this supplemental payment, Rob was furious. He finally agreed, only because he was afraid I might act on my threat to speak to Melissa's husband.

During the next few days, on auto-pilot, I followed the rest of the attorney's suggestions, giving him the information he needed and going through what felt like preparations for a funeral.

How to Act During Negotiations and in Court

"Get in there and act like a man—you will garner his respect—you will do the best with him right after he's dumped you—later when the other woman gets into the act, you will get less[24]*."* Sally Warren, *Dumped*

This is definitely the time to put on your business hat. No histrionics, no lust for revenge, no self-doubts, no attempt to curry favor by being the "good little girl," no being the victim, no giving up because you feel you do not have a chance, just you—being straightforward, there to get what is yours, to handle your business with as little emotion as possible.

If attempts at resolution fail, then you will wind up in court, a stressful and expensive experience. Attorney Dan Butler says the three things you need to go through a litigated divorce are control over your emotions, therapeutic counseling and legal strategy.

Your lawyer is not a therapeutic counselor. This is business; go to him with questions. Do not be afraid of looking like a bitch. Look like a lawyer, act like a lawyer.

The online Chicago Personal Injury Lawyer Guide[25] has assessed the typical mistakes frequently made by parties involved in court actions. They point out that individuals heading into the legal system often have no true perspective on what the likely outcome of their case may be.

This website explains that participants fall into two categories. The first are those who believe they are entitled to much more, than they may be. They may have an expectation that their situation warrants the court's favor when it actually may not. The other extreme seen is that of the person who feels defeated before she goes to court. This person does not expect to gain anything and expects to lose everything. Both these extremes of confidence can lead to big, irreversible mistakes.

A second problem is the highly charged emotions that accompany divorce. The emotions of anger, hurt, grief and jealousy can be so overwhelming that they make sane, logical decision-making impossible. If you find yourself in one of these states, put off any major life decisions you feel compelled to make. Get away from your situation to get perspective. Even a weekend away can help you to get a clearer perspective on things. Try to keep a larger, long-term perspective. Ask yourself, "What is the most important long-term outcome I need?" Use counselors, attorneys and other advisors to help you with those decisions that must be made now.

Along those same lines, your emotions may lead you to do things that can work against you in the divorce process. Acting out of emotion now can make you look bad and impair your ability to get a fair settlement (as well as alienate those who are on your side and want to help you). Do not become your own worst enemy.

Any documents presented to you during this time must be read and considered thoughtfully. This is hard to do. You may want to just sign off and be done with it—or not read the fine print—but take the time to do this right. Sign no documents, agree to nothing until you have had a chance to discuss with others and think it over. Don't hesitate to inform your lawyer of any discrepancies or mistakes that need correcting; feel free to ask questions. All of the above are reasons why the right attorney's advice at the earliest stage of your divorce is so critical to your outcome.

How to Act in Court

Hopefully, you will be able to work out a settlement without going to court. But if that does not happen, and the thought of speaking out in court is nerve wracking, you might ask your doctor for a mild tranquilizer. Make sure you try it out before your court date. It will probably help to have a friend or relative accompany you. In court be respectful and calm. You are neither a victim nor the victor. Do not try to please your ex by trying to be easy in the settlement arena. He will respect you more if you treat your relationship with him as you would a business relationship. Put on your big girl panties, straighten your back, and think of yourself as a negotiator, not a dumped, forlorn lover waiting to get a tossed a few bones.

Chapter 12
My Husband Leaves

"Where you used to be, there is a hole in the world, which I find myself constantly walking around in the daytime, and falling in at night."
Edna St. Vincent Millay

My husband flew to one of his client's homes out-of-state and made plans to move to that city. It would put him very close to Melissa, but far enough that it would not look suspicious to her husband. She told my husband that they could not live together until after her husband died. How decent of her.

With my attorney's help, I had legal separation papers completed. My leverage was that he wanted me to have no contact with his new love—rather no contact with her husband, who still was in the dark. My husband said that Melissa was upset with him for admitting to me that they had actually had intercourse.

As I said before, Melissa had told him she married her husband (who was also more than 10 years older than she) only because he was sick and needed her help. That she did not love him but would stay with him until he died. Then she and Rob could be together. My cynical mind concluded that she wanted to inherit from her husband and then have mine waiting in the wings.

My husband later asked me if he could come home to have an operation so I could take care of him. He suggested that he come home for Thanksgiving and Christmas too as Melissa would have to spend that with her husband and, after all, he and I both would be alone. It seemed to make perfect sense to him. I said, "And you would then go back to her after the holidays, right? Do you understand what that would do to me emotionally?" No, he did not. I could not fathom how he thought that might be acceptable. I declined.

Instead, I wept and wept. I had to take every picture of him down so I could not see him; not see him or any of his belongings. His handkerchiefs that I had carefully folded brought me to tears. A letter he had written me, his key chain, his gloves—all brought me to my knees with grief. My 20-year marriage was over. The primary focus of my life, what I sacrificed for, worked for, was devoted to for 20 years had been taken from me by his and another woman's selfish desires.

This ending, like most endings to marriages, did not happen overnight. There was, on my part, ambivalence. I still loved him. We had 20 good years—not just OK years, but good years. He had lots of great qualities. What made it all impossible was his obvious obsession with this other woman. He showed me that his priority was the relationship he had with her, not me, not our years together, not our family.

Leaving the House

In my experience, love is always dangerous ground and no more so than when it goes bad. You may want to leave. You may not want to see that creep again ever. You may even be afraid of him. But do not be the one to leave unless you feel you are in physical danger and are unable to get a restraining order.

Possession gives you leverage. If you leave, you will be at a financial disadvantage as you have to support a new residence. If you are the one who leaves, your spouse may claim desertion. You may have a better chance of keeping the house if you stay in it. If you have children, a judge may tend to want to leave the children in the same house they have been in all along.

Getting Out Safely

You may think it impossible that your spouse would harm you. But all you have to do is watch the news to know that passion, anger, greed, lust and jealousy can lead seemingly normal people to do horrible things to their spouses and children. Never underestimate what your mate or ex-mate may do. If you know or suspect your spouse may hurt you or your children then you must take precautions to protect yourself.

If you don't think it can happen to you, read Annie's story.

Annie's Story

Annie came from a small Midwestern town and met her husband-to-be, a young, dashing, Air Force lieutenant, at a college dance. He was from Los Angeles, a world away. He was fast-talking, charismatic, smart and strong. He swept her off her feet…he was truly her first love. They had a passionate courtship, a traditional wedding and then he was sent overseas. In between tours in Asia, when they saw each other, the reunion was always passionate.

As their relationship developed, she saw little red flags. On their honeymoon, he went into a store to pay for gas. Annie found another woman's name and telephone number in the glove compartment of the car. It was clear from what was written on the note that her husband had met this woman at one of those same college dances after they had become engaged. She asked him about it and he could not explain why he had it and the doubts began. When Annie asked him about his past relationships she did not like the answers. His past relationships with women seemed callous. She had concerns about his character.

He began to consistently lie about things. Over time, Annie caught him in many small lies. Like most women, she could remember what he had said much better than he could. She began to cross-question him.

Things became tense between them, especially when she caught him lying. On these occasions, he would leave for a few hours or a few days. Once, while visiting her parents' home, he got up in the middle of the night and left…no note, nothing. She came down to breakfast the next morning and he was gone. She was scared and heart-broken. They got back together after that and started seeing a marriage counselor. She kept asking herself and her friends, "What am I doing wrong? Is it me?" Friends watching this assured her it was not her fault.

The night she found condoms in his travel bag was the end. "I asked him if he was having an affair. He said no. We went to a marriage counselor, a woman he chose. But he was still cheating and the counselor knew that but did not tell me. I found out later and felt I had been duped in the counseling sessions."

When Annie would question or confront him, they would argue and he then began to physically abuse her. It started with a backhanded slap in the face. She was stunned. She had never experienced any type of abuse from parents, friends, etc. in her life. She left the house under duress one night and stayed with friends.

They split up and reunited many times. He wanted the separations but could not stand the thought that she might go out with other men. After the final separation he began stalking her. He asked others to spy on her. He was able to get a copy of the key to her new apartment. One night as she was showering, he let himself in, dragged her out of the bathroom and raped her. She was too afraid to report him.

Terrified, she moved out of state and was able to recover her life with the support of friends. She would never have dreamed that this type of relationship could have happened to her. Her advice to others would be to "really get to know the person you are dating and considering marrying… because physical chemistry is not as important as mutual values…find out what his values really are."

If your Spouse is Abusive

If your spouse has abused you verbally or physically in the past, you can expect that that behavior will increase. Abusers want control and your desire to leave, take the children and split your material assets will certainly accelerate his need to control you.

- Leave your home immediately before the violence escalates uncontrollably. Go to friends or relatives and ask them not to share any information about your whereabouts. Put geographic distance between you if possible. Visit your nearest crisis center if you have no other viable options. For a list of crisis centers around the country, search the National Coalition Against Domestic Violence Web site (see Resources below). You can also call (800) 799-SAFE to find a crisis center near you.

- Change your cell or home phone number immediately after you've escaped the situation.

- Document any attempts at contact by the perpetrator and save any threatening phone messages or photographs that show injuries at the hands of the abuser. This is your evidence should you decide to press charges or file a restraining order.

- Make an escape plan in the event the abuser discovers where you're staying. Avoid any route that takes you through rooms with potential weapons, such as the kitchen.

- Change your everyday routine. Take a new route to work or leave your home at a different time every day. These changes may help prevent your abuser from stalking you.

- Speak with a family law advocate at your local crisis center. He or she can help you press charges against the perpetrator, file a temporary restraining order and advise you on how to seek a permanent restraining order.

- Arrange to meet the abuser in a public place, if necessary. While it's best to avoid the abuser completely, if you must exchange documents or personal effects, do it in broad daylight where plenty of people are around. Even better, have some friends make the exchange for you or ask them to accompany you if you must meet with the abuser.

These suggestions and more are from the Web site: http://www.ehow.com/how_2036866_escape-domestic-violence.html

A Success Story

You may feel your situation is hopeless. You may feel overwhelmed, but many women have come out of very tough situations and been able to create great new lives for themselves.

This is Kara's story. If you marry young there is a double vulnerability to your situation. Kara met her husband to be when she was just 17, at a McDonald's on Valentine's Day. To her, that meeting had special meaning because of the holiday. She brought her new boyfriend home to meet her parents. Her father in particular was suspicious. Her boyfriend was five years older in age and seemed much older than that in experience.

After a whirlwind courtship of nine months, she was deeply in love. He acted like a perfect gentleman, but it was just that: an act. Her father was so concerned about her boyfriend's character that he finally took out a restraining order against him. "But, I was in love. We snuck out one night and eloped and got married."

In Kara's own words: "Once we were married, he began to control everything I did. I could not wear anything he did not like, no short skirts. He did not like my friends and did his best to drive them away. He did not want me to go to college. I tried but he made it so difficult. He finally moved us out of state to live next door to his parents, I think to just get me away from my parents, family and friends."

"He did not want to have children. But, I got pregnant. That was the first time he hit me. I begged him not to—I was afraid he would hurt the baby. I told him my father would kill him if he hit me. He paused; then threw me against the wall. I got pregnant again. He did not abuse the children and was careful to hit me and threaten me when we were alone. At one point I found a picture in his things. The picture was of his first wife. She had two black eyes. That helped me to know it was not me. For 18 years I stayed with this man suffering from his emotional, physical and verbal abuse and threats."

Ironically, part of the reason Kara stayed was her feeling that her family would disapprove of her leaving her husband. When she did make her move they applauded it.

"When the boys were 13 and 17, a friend of mine, who also had an abusive husband, just up and left him. She had no job and no place to go but she just did it. When I saw that, I said, 'I can do this. I can leave,' and I knew if I did not leave then I might never have the confidence. He had told me he would never allow me to leave him, never agree to a divorce and most importantly, he would never allow me to take the children."

"So, I left. It was the hardest thing I ever did, to leave without my children. I was not afraid he would hurt them. I tried to explain to them. Tad would not listen, he was 13. James, who was 17, understood. For three months I lived in hiding. When he finally found where I was living, he came and sat outside my place to intimidate me. Finally, he got another woman. I had made it; but was terrified he would come and get me. For nine years after I left, I kept a box of evidence. The picture of his first wife with the black eyes, pictures that proved his infidelity, other things."

She was only able to burn it all when she married again.

"The next man in my life, Brad, spent a lot of time teaching me to get what I needed and wanted. He helped me become the woman I was before I got married," she continued. Kara's story has a happy ending. She got close to her boys again. The older one came and lived with her. They are now grown and she has grandchildren to play with. Her Brad died. But, she has found herself another man who is her husband, lover and best friend.

Domestic Violence Hotlines and Help
National Domestic Violence Hotline: 1-800-799-SAFE (7233) or
1-800-787-3224 (TTY)—A crisis intervention and referral phone line for domestic violence. (Texas Council on Family Violence)

State Coalition List—Directory of state offices that can help you find local support, shelter, and free or low-cost legal services. Includes all states, as well as the District of Columbia, Puerto Rico, and the Virgin Islands. (National Coalition against Domestic Violence)

http://safeharborshelter.com/- Located in Richmond, VA, providing a variety of services for abused women.

Chapter 13
Helping Your Children Get through a Divorce

"The worst mistakes people make when divorcing are: they fail to get a good lawyer. And if there's a lover, they flaunt him, making their spouse act crazy, prolonging the process and costing them a bundle. They hide assets, which will be found—also extremely expensive. Or they put the kids in the middle, which just makes them heinous human beings."[26]
Gerald Nissenbaum, divorce attorney

Despite the fact that my sons were grown up, they were devastated when my husband told them about our separation. We had married when they were 4 and 11. As children, they had accepted him with open arms and trusted him implicitly. He was their stepfather but had become as close as if he was their real father.

They could not believe he had been unfaithful; they could not comprehend him leaving me. The older one wept openly. The younger one was full of anger. The hardest part was seeing their belief in him shattered. Divorce may mean heartbreak or relief for you, but what about the children? Is there any way you can make that better? Here are the perspectives of some children whose parents have divorced and what they would like you to know.

Children of Divorce Speak

Jennifer Roberts, her husband and four children (Suzanne, 16; Rose, 14; Daniel, 7; and Marie, 4) and their beagle, Odie, lived next door to her parents, giving her children easy access to the added support and affection of their grandparents. The children's school was within walking distance. But all that changed when she and her husband, after years of attempts at keeping their marriage together, finally separated.

From the children's perspective there had been cold wars and hot spells of fighting between their parents for years, so they did not expect anything to happen. But, one summer, three years ago, the two eldest girls,

Suzanne and Rosemarie returned from summer camp to find their bedrooms painted and redecorated. Their parents seemed to be in harmony—they were surprised and pleased. But shortly after, their parents told them they would be getting a divorce.

"It was a surprise but not a surprise," Rosemarie said. "They had problems for years. We knew they were considering divorce, but it always seemed so distant, then suddenly, there it was. We had to move." She missed having her grandparents next door and was afraid she would have to choose between her parents. She was afraid for the two youngest children, Daniel and Marie.

"The reality did not hit me until the day we moved. I was just standing there in the house with all these people coming in and out, moving things. It was awful."

Liz was five when her parents divorced. Because they could not afford to separate, her parents continued to live together. "I really did not understand what was going on at all. I was too young. I guess they were trying to protect me." Then they moved in with their grandmother. Her father moved in with his girlfriend. Liz said, "That is when I realized what the divorce really meant."

Marie Louise, whose parents divorced when she was 13, said, "Initially, I was OK with my parents divorcing. I thought that should happen. It wasn't a big emotional thing for me." However, her mom had to move to a new city and go to work full time.

Suddenly, Marie found herself with the added responsibility of taking care of two younger siblings, one of whom was handicapped. She said, "I went from a very structured life to one with no structure and more responsibility. So I rebelled. I went off on jaunts with my girlfriends. Once, we hitchhiked to Maryland. I would stay out late at night, disobey in every way. My mother could not stop me."

Finally her mother had someone from their church give her some tough love. "He was onto my every trick and let me have it when I stepped over the line." She added, "That brought me back to reality. He gave me the structure I needed."

Sometimes, the non-custodial parent feels the children do not need him anymore; that they are busy with their new lives, and so that parent pulls away. After the divorce, Rosemarie said her dad did keep in contact for awhile but then the visits diminished. Her brother Daniel said," I wish my dad would let me help him at work again like he used to." His sister Suzanne added, "It's a bad feeling. Sometimes we don't hear from him for weeks." Children need and want to keep both parents in their lives.

Couples coaches David Hulbert and Sherry Finneran of the Family Education Center in Richmond, Va., suggest that even if your spouse is not cooperating, try to keep the line of communication open for your kids' sake. "Do not say negative things about your spouse. The child is one-half you and one-half your spouse. It makes them feel bad about themselves if they have a bad impression of their father or mother."

Daniel added, "I'm glad my mom is not mean to my dad like some of my friends parents are to each other."

If you are a stepparent, take it slow. Your relationship with the children must progress naturally and cannot be forced. George, who was 9 years old when his parents divorced, said he loved both parents and was sad. "I got a new stepfather. The best thing my mom did was to tell him to be a friend to my brother and me and not try to be a dad." Liz said she could not respond to her father's new wife. "She tried to be friendly with me, but I blamed her for their divorce and could not accept her; perhaps if she had taken it slower; not tried so hard, so fast."

David and Sherry remark, "As hard as it may be, build a relationship with your ex's new friend. That person will be handling your child during visits. You want them as a friend or at least neutral not an enemy."

One thing several children also mentioned was their wish that the old family could participate together in school events and be together on holidays. This requires acceptance on the part of both stepparents. David, who was four when his parents divorced, said, "It was immensely important to me that we could still all be together on different occasions, my birthday parties, school and sports events and some holidays." Liz said, "One thing I wished was that we could have had times together like a family, my mom, dad and my brothers and me after the divorce."

Other things that kids wish their parents knew include, "No checklists, a visit should be a visit. No lists of 'are you doing everything right.' "

Giving your child special time—just you and him or her—is cherished. Liz said, "My dad took us out on Wednesdays. He picked us up and took my brothers to their Boy Scout meetings. He and I went to the library and picked out books. This was my favorite day of the week and my best times with him."

This book does not begin to cover what you need to know about helping your children get through a divorce, but there are certain principles that most childcare professionals, counselors, attorneys and children who have gone through this agree on. Childcare professionals[27] suggest the following 12 ways you can help children during divorce:

Twelve Ways to Help your Children During a Divorce:

1) Do, If at all possible, tell them with both parents present.
2) Do not tell them about an affair, if there was one.
3) Assure them that they are not responsible.
4) Assure them it's the parent's decision and they are not responsible—they cannot change the outcome.
5) Assure them that both parents still love them.
6) Give concrete info about how their lives will stay the same and how they may change.
7) Do not ask them to take sides or make them your confidante.
8) Give them permission to stay friends with the leaving parent and new family.
9) If at all possible, be in agreement with your ex on children's behavior.
10) Maintain as many traditions, customs and activities as possible.
11) Keep promises. Do what you say you will do.
12) Tell them that your home will always be their home.

Part V
Security

Chapter 14
Security in an Insecure World

"It is not the strongest of the species that survives, nor the most intelligent that survives. It is the one that is the most adaptable to change."
Charles Darwin

Every morning was black—the color black. I did not want to get up. There was no reason to. My world had collapsed and not just by chance, but through betrayal and lies. Through the deliberate machinations of a woman who wanted my husband as an accessory, a tool in her life. And he, he was willing to throw me away, with no concern about my fate. I had some cash and I had the house, but even so, I would need additional income to keep my head above water.

With my previous work history, references and contacts, I was able to get a number of interviews. They took notes, brought in their marketing teams to hear my ideas for their companies, but I got no offers. Finally, one woman business owner put it to me bluntly, "Isabelle, you are sixty. How do you expect to compete with these young guys right out of college? You can't."

So I could not get hired. I was still doing some of the bookkeeping for the business and received income for three months for this work. When I asked my ex about the fact that he had left me at 60—that I had no income and no job prospects, he said, "What do you want? I kept you on the payroll for three months." What I got for 20 years of devoted personal and professional care was three months' severance pay and my alimony bonus.

I looked at working for a medical tourism company. It would pay commission-only based on sales, but I had done that kind of work before. Eventually, I decided not to follow that path but had, in the meantime, acquired a huge amount of information on that business.

One evening, I was sharing this with a friend at the YMCA who publishes a medical journal. He said, "that is really interesting. Write me an article about it for the journal." Medical journals do not pay, but it is a feather in your cap to be published in one and I had nothing else to do.

The article took months to write because it needed great detail, that the sources had to be perfect, and there could be absolutely no mistakes. It went back and forth between the editor and me.

In the meantime, I had the idea to pitch the same topic with a different perspective to a local magazine. One of those freebies that you get in the grocery store; but it was and is an excellent periodical with lots of readers. To my amazement, the editor took it—not only that, but he complimented me on it. "Well written, well documented, interesting…"

I began to write other articles, one about exercise at the YMCA, then about health, then internet dating—onward and upward. They were getting accepted and I was getting paid. Not much, not enough to survive on, but it was a start. And, it was work I loved. Seeing my name in a printed byline restored some of my flattened ego. So, I clung to the writing like a life preserver.

Money

Being married can mean that you have emotional and financial security. But, as illustrated above, it can also mean that you merely have the illusion of security.

Unfortunately, at the time when you most need to feel some sense of stability, your financial situation may make you completely insecure. Again, it is all about adaptation. The quicker you come to the realization that you need to either bring in more income or cut your expenses, the less painful it will all be and the less chance you will get into trouble.

So what to do about your new situation? Will you be OK financially? Are you due alimony or child support? Do you have the means to pursue your ex if he does not pay? You may want to consider a lump sum for alimony instead of monthly payments if possible. After all, what if he loses his job, skips town or dies?

In more than one case, women I spoke with let their ex get away with not paying child support because they wanted the husband to continue to have a positive relationship with the child, keep to a visitation schedule and maintain a peaceful relationship with the ex. I am not suggesting you do this—just saying that you might have a higher priority than alimony or child support, and if you do that is fine.

If you need more money, you can either cut expenses or increase income.

Are there places you can cut back? The biggest expense is your home or apartment. This should not be more than 25 percent of your income. Trying to stay in the same house may result in you having to cut everything else in your life style. Consider the possibility of moving back with parents or moving in with a friend or relative.

Or, stay in your home and rent out a room to someone else who is in the same boat as you. I know at least four people who have rented out rooms in their homes as a result of divorce, (including myself.) This is not such a big adaptation as you may think. It is all about finding the right person and having rules that you stick to. Getting a credit report online is easy. Make sure you get two month's rent up-front as insurance so you won't have to pay out of pocket for damage or absorb skipped rent.

Are you over 62? You can apply for your own social security benefits or for half of your spouse's (if you were married for ten years or more.) Call the social security office. They can tell you how much half of your spouse's amount will be and whether that is more or less than your predicted amount. If your ex dies, you can apply for all of his benefits.

Other quick ways to generate cash include cashing in a life insurance policy or bonds, refinancing your mortgage, selling stuff on Craig's list, changing your withholding, boosting rates of return on savings or CDs by comparing rates, looking for higher returns on stock dividends—and yes, you could plant your own victory garden.

There are innumerable entrepreneurial ways to increase income. Tutoring kids in the evening? Babysitting children who are the same age as yours achieves two objectives: your children get company and you get income. Always wanted to make and sell something? This is an opportunity to try something without a critical spouse undermining you. Look around, what is needed in your neighborhood? Also look at the most ROI (return on investment) you can get for your time and effort. Always make sure your product can be sold at a price that covers your costs and nets you a reasonable profit for your efforts. Local SCORE offices can help you set up a business and even provide some mentoring.

What skills do you have? Need new skills? You can take computer courses for free at some neighborhood libraries or for a low cost at community colleges. Look for job training opportunities and by all means try to do something you like, love, or are good at.

Child Support

Most states have child support enforcement agencies to help you collect whatever support the court orders. Most states and counties will also assist you in utilizing all manner of public records to locate your ex and/or his assets. Look to county property records and tax offices to garnish wages, attach liens to property or bank accounts. Even the local department of motor vehicles will help you get information and, I hope, cash. There is also the national non-profit group the Association for Children for the Enforcement of Child Support, which can provide advice on how to collect child support. See: http://www.cocommunity.net/agency/aces-assoc-children-enforcement-child-support.html

Managing Money

Is managing money a new skill for you? Or have you had trouble in the past? Getting a credit card in your own name is essential but remember, virtually every financial guru says to absolutely limit your use of credit cards-do not use them to get through months where your income is low. You will never get out from under them. It is essential to save and apportion money. T. Harve Eker[28] in his book on money management outlines a simple system called "**The Jar System.**"

The Jar System consists of taking your income and dividing it into six jars. Those jars would consist of the following:

1) A Financial Freedom Account (10%): Saved off the top of your salary or income, preferably automatically.
2) Long Term Savings for Spending (10%): Big purchases, car replacement, auto repairs, home repairs, appliances.
3) Education (10%): For yourself, to improve your ability to earn.
4) Necessities (55%): Rent, food, utilities, medical bills.
5) Play Money (10%): Entertainment and trips, etc.
6) Give (5%): Charity

You can create your own jar system based on your priorities. The important part is the concept of setting aside money for future use and not living paycheck-to-paycheck, no matter what sacrifices that may take.

Based on my experience, there are other things that make for real security. In addition to the usual things we think of as assets, such as streams of Income, money in the bank, real estate, automobiles, stocks, bonds, jewelry, artwork, antiques and things that can be sold, there are other assets just as important.

Your friends, family, relatives, coworkers, employees, those people who make up your personal and professional network, are an invaluable asset. Professional associations, clubs, memberships and networks can answer your questions, help you solve problems, help you find a new job, a new partner, childcare or get you to the right doctor. You should create a personal network of advisors, business consultants, bankers, financial advisors, doctors, lawyers, law enforcement officers, political friends. Think of the people in your life as assets and do your best to expand that network outward. This is not a time to withdraw but a necessary opportunity to expand your circles of influence. These people can get you answers, solve problems and sometimes protect you.

You may also want to start your own mastermind group. A mastermind group is a select few acquaintances who are as smart as or smarter than you. This is definitely not a group for chit-chat or emotional support. You meet at least once a month, share your problems and goals and barriers, then help one another stay focused, find solutions and make progress in life. You use the combined mind skills of your group to overcome problems and challenges in your professional and personal life.

Napoleon Hill, in his famous classic book *Think and Grow Rich* (one of the best-selling books of all time) describes how these think tanks were used by Franklin Roosevelt during the Great Depression. Napoleon Hill, using the advice of Thomas Edison, Andrew Carnegie and Henry Ford, teaches you how to focus on your goals and conceive, believe and achieve them. It is the foundation of most motivational books written during the past century. If you are in business or want to start a business, this concept is a necessity.

Part VI
Emotions of Divorce

Chapter 15
You're Taking this Way too Personally

"I don't know why they call it heartbreak. It feels like every other part of my body is broken too." Missy Altijd

During the time I was going through all this, at one point, someone—yes, it might have been my husband, although I'm not sure—said to me, "You know, you are taking this all way too personally." From my perspective at that time, it was all personal. From my perspective now, it really wasn't about me.

But that is little comfort when your world is tipped upside down. Going through a divorce is one of the worst roller coasters of emotion you can imagine. If your spouse dies, you grieve. If he leaves you under especially ugly circumstances involving choosing someone else over you, financially devastating you, discovering you have been lied to and betrayed, you experience a major loss of trust in the human race in general, anger over the injustice and cruelty of it, jealousy and rage, and sometimes the desire for revenge. In short, you take it all very personally.

When you are dumped by your lover and partner, you lose your sense of self-worth. All your insecurities come to the front of the line: you are not worthy, you never were, your success was all an illusion and now you see the truth that you are not lovable, you are not wanted or needed, you are not attractive, you are old so there is no hope, there is no point in trying, your former life was a masquerade and this lack of everything is the reality that was there all along.

Suddenly Alone

My children were both grown and living far away. My parents were both deceased. My uncle, one of my last remaining relatives, had died three years earlier. My two best friends of 30 years lived hours away and besides, they were in happy, stable, long-term marriages and I could bother them only so much.

My brother, mentally ill and in a hospital in Massachusetts, was dying slowly of colon cancer. I was flying there every other week to see him, and these were depressing and lonely trips. I was trying to minimize his suffering and loneliness while in that same space myself. I could not share with him any of my problems lest they further depress him.

There was no one to greet me when I arrived back in town from these trips. At the airport I watched as many of my fellow travelers were greeted by loved ones. I remembered the many times I had greeted my husband at this same airport, with hugs and kisses, and I cried some more.

It occurred to me that if my plane were lost, no one would realize I was gone for days. There was no one to call and tell about my trip. I had a sense of being adrift in a vast blue ocean with nothing on any horizon in any direction, nothing to hang onto, no one to even call out to—lost—about to be suffocated by the endless vast water that would swallow me up. Did my existence mean nothing?

Divorce and Your Health

A miserable marriage and/or divorce takes its toll on you emotionally but it can also affect you physically. It may be that the extreme emotional stress you experience reduces your immune system's ability to fight off disease.

Joy was in her 30s, working as a full-time nurse and was the mother of a five year old when she developed leukemia. This happened shortly after she found that her suspicions about her husband having an affair were accurate. He refused to acknowledge her illness and was emotionally abusive as he vacillated between Joy and his mistress. She went through the agony of a bone marrow transplant, rallied, but then developed hepatitis from a blood transfusion. While the hepatitis is listed as cause of death, I truly believe her husband's infidelity and mental cruelty helped do her in.

My own cousin **Colleen** married her high school sweetheart, who turned out not to be so sweet after all. She kept thinking if only she tried harder, he would love her more. She had grown up caring for an alcoholic, abusive mother and had little confidence in herself. She was juggling a very difficult, but rewarding job as an LPN and raising three children under the age of eight with no help from her sometimes employed spouse.

The accolades and awards she won for excellence at her job were her only source of self-esteem. She began to have headaches and eye problems.

She was weak. Her doctor, knowing her lifestyle, thought it was overwork. When the headaches became disabling, he ordered a CAT scan. She had a large tumor growing in her head. The diagnosis shocked everyone, the nurses at the hospital where she worked rallied around her. Her only thought was, "Please God, let me live to raise my children."

The surgery was successful in that the tumor, which was benign, was removed. However, during surgery, she suffered a stroke. The left side of her face went slack. Despite the efforts of the doctors, nothing could be done. There was massive damage to the nerves in that side of her face. At age 34, she was permanently disfigured.

Her husband came to see her in the hospital. He took one look and left the room. When she was discharged, he drove her home, helped her inside, and then said, "I can't stand looking at you. I am leaving." She was alone with three children to raise while she recovered from surgery and a stroke. He never paid child support so she raised the children on her LPN pay, working as many hours as she possibly could. (As an aside, many years later, when she was in her 50s, she met a neighbor whose wife had just died. After 20-plus years of not dating, she had a real romance followed by a happy marriage.)

Then, there is Belinda's story. **Belinda** is a 30-something, petite dark-haired Irish lass with a mischievous twinkle in her eye. She is also an oncology registered nurse who, at a very young age, began to carve out a big name for herself as a top researcher at one of the best hospitals in the country. Her skill soon put her in partnership with the chief oncologist at the hospital.

With her help, his number of publications grew and so did his name. They became co-presenters and partners on other levels also. "I was impressed with him, in awe. I could not do enough to help him." They married and had a child. "I thought we had a great partnership and marriage. But after a few years things began to change. He began to pick at me, to criticize me. When we presented together at conferences, he seemed to take all the credit. He treated me badly in front of our colleagues. I wondered what was going on. I was trying very hard for my son's sake to keep the relationship together. One day, during a heated exchange, he told me I was 'nothing."

"I had enough. I wanted to retain some self -respect. So, I left with one suitcase of clothes, the baby and nothing else. He said, 'I will ruin you, I will starve you out.' He gave me no support financially during this time. I gave up the fabulous home we had together. I requested no alimony, none of the furnishings or assets, only child support for the baby. The judge could not believe it. During this time, several of our colleagues and their wives comforted me. One day one said, 'There is something you need to know. He had several girlfriends while you were together. He still does.' While I was 17 years younger than him, his new girlfriend was even younger than me! That was why he was so nasty to me.

"While going through all of this, I began to have a great deal of difficulty with fatigue. I had memory problems, and headaches. I had a headache that lasted three days and went to my doctor. He said, 'It's just stress.' I said, 'I know it is not stress. Something is very wrong with me.' I requested a cat scan. He said it was not necessary. His nurse, who I knew personally, wrote up the referral and signed the doctor's name to it."

"I had the scan and it showed a very large lemon-sized tumor in my brain. The doctor was very apologetic. The surgery that followed was tricky but a success. The tumor was benign. I went through recovery, regained my strength and went back to work. I found out later that my husband's first wife had died of breast cancer. I believe the marriage created an environment of stress and pain that allowed that tumor to beat my immune system. I heard that he cheated on his first wife too. I wondered if the stress she was under with him caused her cancer."

Divorce and Suicide

"You can write me down in history with hateful twisted lies, you can tread me in this very dirt but still, like dust, I'll rise." Maya Angelou

What would you say if I told you that J.K. Rowling, Halle Berry and Oprah Winfree all considered ending their young lives over some miserable man?

One recent study by the National Institute for Healthcare Research in Rockville, Md.,[29] indicates that divorced people are three times as likely to commit suicide as people who are married. The Institute says that divorce now ranks as the No. 1 factor linked with suicide rates in major U.S. cities, ranking above all other physical, financial, and psychological factors.

Long before she became famous, Oprah Winfree, in the midst of a losing love affair, considered suicide. Oprah had been sexually molested as a child by an older male relative. She had been raped at the age of nine. As a teen, she gave birth to an out of wedlock child, who died soon after.

While these would be enough reasons to make her consider ending her life, her closest call came much later when as a young woman, she was involved in a dead-end love affair with a married man. She wrote a suicide note and sent it to a friend. She said of that episode, "I couldn't do it. I was afraid something good might happen in my life and I would miss it."

Of course, later, great things beyond her wildest dreams happened to her. She became one of the most successful TV talk-show hosts ever and amassed a fortune that has allowed her to create all kinds of wonderful projects for others. How different would our world be without Oprah Winfree?

Halle Berry, recently named one of the world's most beautiful women, was also hurt enough after her marriage to baseball player David Justice ended that she almost took her own life.

"I was sitting in my car, and I knew the gas was coming in when I had an image of my mother finding me. She sacrificed so much for her children, and to end my life would be an incredibly selfish thing to do. My sense of worth was so low. I had to reprogram myself to see the good in me. Because someone didn't love me didn't mean I was unlovable. I promised myself I would never be a coward again."

Halle went on to become a superstar with roles as a James Bond Girl with Pierce Brosnan in *"Die Another Day"* and the sleek star of *"Catwoman."* She has made millions, and now has her own child, Nayhla.

J.K. Rowling , the author of the fabulously successful *Harry Potter* series, was at a low point in her 20s after her marriage dissolved. She had no money, no prospects and a small child to raise.

"The thing that made me go for help," said Rowling, "was probably my daughter. She was someone that earthed me, grounded me, and I thought, this isn't right, this can't be right, she cannot grow up with me in this state." Luckily for all the Harry Potter fans, she lived, raised her child, wrote her books and became fabulously wealthy.

Would any of these women have dreamed that their lives would change this much? Did they have a clue as to the great stuff awaiting them? Now, you may not have the fantastic turnaround in your life that these women did, but who knows what wonderful things may happen?

Consider also the story of Buckminster Fuller, who later in life became world-famous as the engineer who designed the geodesic dome. He was suicidal after losing his father-in-law's money in a business deal, followed by the death of his four-year-old daughter.

As he stood on the edge of a lake considering drowning himself, he asked himself, "What could a puny human like me accomplish to make my life worthwhile?" He heard this answer in his head: "You do not have the right to eliminate yourself. You do not belong to you. Your significance will remain forever obscure to you but you may assume you are fulfilling your significance if you apply yourself to converting all your experience to the highest advantage of others."

He did just that. The rest of his life was spent creating unique architectural inventions that solved problems for people all over the world.

The Web site metanoia.org/suicide explains that suicidal feelings begin when the pain in our lives exceeds our pain-coping resources. It is simply an imbalance of pain versus coping resources that can be corrected.[30]

Think about how your death might impact people you love, such as your children, your parents, and your friends. List all the good qualities you have and all the people who have loved you. Think about the possible good things that might come your way in the future. Think about the good you might do for others in the future, about dreams you have that could come true. Whatever you are going through—you can get through it.

Most of us do not realize the reality of suicide. We may think of it in a romantic way, as a way to express our feelings dramatically or end our pain forever. I worked in brain injury for several years and saw a number of people who had attempted suicide through a car crash, a gun or a drug overdose. They did not die but lived with damaged brains and limbs. The ones I saw were destined to spend the rest of their lives in assisted-living facilities or nursing homes.

Ending life is never simple. It's messy, difficult and unpredictable in its results. Not to minimize your pain but simply to bring home to you the gory realities of suicide, let me repeat Dorothy Parker's poem: "Razors pain you, rivers are damp, acids stain you, and drugs cause cramp, guns aren't lawful, nooses give, gas smells awful, you might as well live."

If you are thinking of suicide, you should first of all put off for at least 24 hours any plans to end your life. Then talk to others. Having a counselor, a network of friends, or relatives who can listen, is critical. They are part of your pain-coping resources.

Don't give yourself the additional burden of trying to deal with this alone. Just talking about how you got to where you are releases a lot of pressure, and it might be just the additional coping resource you need to regain your balance. If you do not want to share your suicidal thoughts with someone you know, then please call a suicide hotline.

Resources for Those with Thoughts of Suicide
- Call the National Suicide Prevention Lifeline: call 1-800-273-TALK (8255)
- Teenagers, call Covenant House Nine Line: 1-800-999-9999
- Check the front of your phone book for a local crisis line
- Carefully choose a friend or a minister or rabbi you can call, someone who is likely to listen

Connecting Past Trauma Doubles the Pain
Heartache is pain; a pain that feels like it will never go away. One of the elements that can make a loss like death, divorce or separation from a loved even more difficult to bear is when the current loss connects in your subconscious with a past traumatic event.

In my case, a year or so after my husband and I separated, I misplaced a pearl necklace that I treasured. I had been packing for a trip. I did not want to risk taking the pearls with me and hid them in the house. Unfortunately it was after midnight when I did that and I was pretty much asleep.

When I returned from the trip I had no memory of where I might have hidden them. I knew they were in the house somewhere but a tear-it-apart session did not reveal them. In desperation, I went to a friend who was a hypnotherapist and asked her to put me under to see if I could recall the memory of hiding them.

During the session, she asked me a simple question: "Was there a time in your life when you lost something very important to you?" For some reason that question triggered a memory of my father separating from my mother when I was seven years old. That event was so disturbing to me at that time that I began sleepwalking at night and was found outside the house in my nightgown, searching in my sleep for my father, who was gone. I had not thought about this event consciously since I was a child. As I told her about this, with a floodgate of tears pouring down, I immediately realized that my husband leaving was, in my mind, replaying the same event.

If you have experienced a trauma such as abuse, neglect, abandonment, or lost a parent or someone you were dependent on as a child, you may be equating this divorce to that event. You may experience once again becoming that child in pain. If you can dredge that memory up, do it—then look it full in the face. Realize that when it happened you were vulnerable, fragile and helpless but that now you are strong, independent and capable. You have the ability now to regain control of your life. As a child you had no control. You will remind yourself that you can handle this, you can make your life better and you now have the power you did not have then to bring more people into your life and to have your needs met.

If you can make this connection and come away with a resolution to those past traumas, you will have grown by leaps and bounds and be much better prepared to be a mature adult in a new relationship instead of a wounded child.

In the meantime, below are some simple techniques to get you through your agony days.

First Aid for Heartache

"It is only through disruptions and confusion that we grow, jarred out of ourselves by the collision of someone else's private world with our own." Joyce Carla Oates

Here is my list of first aid measures for loneliness, grief and depression. The brain is a machine, simply that. You can change the state of your mind temporarily or permanently. As a person who has had depressive episodes throughout her life, I can appreciate the necessity of dealing with depression aggressively, as though it were an injury. The suggestions below sound silly, but they do help.

- First and foremost, you may not have anyone, except perhaps your dog and children, telling you they love you. Each morning before you get out of bed, tell yourself, "I love you." Say it with feeling. Tell yourself how great you are. List what you like about yourself and what you feel good about in your life. List what you are grateful for, what you still have and what you can still do. Do this again before you go to bed. Your subconscious will pick up on it even if you do not consciously believe it.

- If the holidays are coming, you may want to plan to have a house full of guests. If you know others who are alone at this time, invite them to be with you. Wrangling an invite to visit your out-of-town friends or relatives is another option. If that is not feasible, plan a trip away where you can pretend it is not Christmas or New Year's Eve.

- Remember when you had a new puppy and you were told to give him a blanket and ticking clock? The idea was that the rhythmic ticking mimicked the beat of a heart, making the puppy feel he was not alone. Well, a heating pad can do the same for you. Your subconscious will interpret that extra heat as if it were another body next to yours. It may enhance your ability to sleep alone at night.

- Speaking of puppies—what else gives you unlimited love, affection and companionship? All that is required is your care and attention for an unlimited supply of positive emotions (and possibly protection). If you ever considered getting a pet, now is a great time.

- Caring for others can make you see the real value you have. Caring for others as a hospital volunteer or at a homeless shelter or food bank can give you perspective on your own situation.

- Ever take care of a baby, preferably a toddler? It is an all-absorbing activity that does not allow you to think about anything else. The act of caring for babies or children allows you to give love and have that love reciprocated unconditionally. You can help care for a friend's child for free or get paid for it—lots of opportunities here. It's easy to find people who need help with their children.

- The last weekend my husband was at home he stayed on the phone with his mistress despite the fact that he was moving out of state and it would be the last weekend we would ever see each other. I felt like I might just go insane. I left the house in tears. I went to a local movie theatre and bought a ticket for an action thriller. This theatre had 14 different movies playing. I watched one, letting myself get as absorbed as possible in the action. After it was over, I did not want to go home. I wanted to stay as completely out of touch with reality as I could. I went into another gallery and watched a movie about a Chihuahua that goes to Hollywood. Then I watched "*Tropic Thunder*," a comedy. I found myself laughing for the first time in weeks. After that, I saw a fantasy film for children. After that, I watched "Tropic

Thunder" again. I stayed in the theatre from noon through the evening until the theatre finally closed around midnight. I asked a friend if I could sleep on her couch that night. The movie marathon was a mentally refreshing experience that took me out of this world for awhile. I believe it may have prevented me from having a nervous breakdown that weekend. So experiences that take you completely out of your box are very helpful.

• Music and dance have the power to change your emotional state in an instant. I set a clock CD player to play Reggae music first thing in the morning because I found that beat in particular lifted my mood and enabled me to get out of bed when I was at my worst. There are many dance venues that require no partner. Line dancing and traditional dance are two forms that are great fun, no partner required.

• Gardening is another healing experience. Making things grow, being close to the creation of nature, is wonderful for the soul.

• Support Groups—If you are like me you may have believed you would never need or benefit from one of these- but a divorce support group can help you more than you can imagine.

Revenge

"Anyone who's been through a divorce will tell you that at one point they have thought murder. The line between thinking murder and doing murder isn't that major." Oliver Stone

After my husband left, my daughter-in-law gave me a copy of the book *First Wives Club*[31]. I read the book, hoping to find something I could relate to in it. The book is the ultimate fantasy for the dumped wife. Three best friends get together to not only honor a friend who commits suicide because her husband leaves her but also to avenge themselves on their wretched exes.

They must first go through a period of really examining themselves. Then, having achieved that growth, they combine their energies and skills. They are able not only to execute exquisite and appropriate revenge on each ex-husband but also to rebuild their own self-esteem and power through their relationships with one another. The book is still on my shelf. Although it's fiction, it gave me a strange sense of comfort during that time. It described a way to reclaim self-esteem and hope for a future in which balance would be restored in my world.

You say you are having fantasies of terrible things happening to your ex? You say that one of the only pleasures in your life is coming up with scenarios in which your ex and his new woman meet with a horrible fate, hopefully one in which you have had a part? This is completely normal and may be indulged in from time to time to help you keep your sanity.

The need for revenge comes from two places. First, you need to feel there is some justice in the scheme of things. To think that when you have done so much for someone and treated them so well only to be betrayed and discarded by them makes you feel as though the world is out of balance. You have a need to restore the balance and thus, achieve a sense that justice has been done. It is not by accident that we call revenge "getting even."

Secondly, being stomped on makes you feel like you have lost all control of your life. Someone has taken it from you. Actually, a lot of our feelings of control are just that: feelings. We really have less control over life than we think. But, revenge gives you the possibility to regain that control; a feeling that you can have an impact.

Counselor's Comment on Revenge:

In most cases, believe it or not, whatever actions you take to get revenge, you will later look on with some embarrassment. What seemed like a great idea at the time will now seem a juvenile prank. So, here are some reasons not to proceed with your plans for revenge.

Attorney Andrea Stiles says to keep the "quiet threat" if you have one. She tells the story of a woman who wanted her husband's boss to know about his affair with his secretary and his plans to divorce her. Her attorney advised against spilling the beans. Andrea said, "First of all, what does it get her? If he loses his job, that will not help her get support or alimony. Also she is giving away leverage she has—what can she get for holding back this information? It is a possible negotiating tool."

The woman told the boss anyway. He did not fire the husband or the secretary, the wife felt like a fool, and the divorce process became an even bigger nightmare.

I discussed the topic of handling your emotions—specifically anger and revenge—with Richmond-based family consultants and educators Sherry Finnerman and David Hulbert.

They said, "Revenge hurts you because it makes you someone you are not. You are giving away yourself. It can also turn others in your drama against you. It takes away your position as the wronged person. You go from being the victim to the aggressor. You can appear to be unhinged."

It also shows they are in control of your life, not you. Staying obsessed with anger can distract you from what you really need to be focused on to survive. It will show in your relationships with others and push them away.

Some of their suggestions to help heal are pretty basic, but easy to forget at a time like this. They said, "Stay healthy. Diet, exercise, stay busy, get support, find something you always wanted to do, weed out toxic people in your life and don't make any big decisions." Real health comes from separating yourself from your emotions—especially anger—and seeing things as they really are.

Sherry added, "Do not speak out against your spouse to your children. They are half you and half their father. Children need to believe in both their parents. Do not make them take sides." Sons in particular may feel bad about themselves when they feel their fathers are "bad." Keep communication open for the children's sake. As for the other woman, you may be sharing your children with her in the future. If you must confront her, wait till you are in control and alone with her. Don't do it in anger.

Most importantly, do not do anything that hurts you, your career or your future. If you do, you are adding more injustice to your side of the scales. The best revenge truly is living well. If it is any consolation, it is said that men who leave their wives for younger women frequently die earlier than they would otherwise. It happens often that if he dumped you for her, he will also dump her for someone else.

The bottom line is that you are spending your precious mental energy in a negative place; wasting time and energy on a process that will give you momentary satisfaction but not improve your life in the long term in any way. Most negative actions can backfire, sometimes resulting in unintended consequences. Your job now is to improve your life and your chances for happiness. That's where your focus needs to be.

The arena in which you can and should exercise your strength and rights is the legal arena. To the best of your ability, have your rights honored. If you are going to court, focus on making that a successful experience. Get as much financial support and assets as you can. Getting more will be increasingly hard as time goes on.

Jeanie's Story

Having said all that, here is one story of revenge to warm your heart. It is a true story relayed to me by a male friend.

A woman he knew—let's say her name was Jeanie—was married to a man who was always finding fault with her. We'll call him Buster. They were both middle-aged and had been married for more than a decade. Buster finally left Jeanie, telling her as he walked out the door that she was a loser.

Jeanie knew that Buster was writing ads in the personal section of the paper, looking for someone more worthy of his attention. He had actually drafted some of these before he left. She looked and immediately recognized his ego-driven description of himself.

Jeanie answered the ad, telling him that she was a model. She explained that she could not give him her phone number as she lived with her mother who forbade her to date. In a later letter, she included a picture of another woman who was a real model, young and gorgeous. Buster, in his letters to her, was wild with excitement. He was desperate to meet her.

Jeanie, pretending to be the model, set up a rendezvous at a local restaurant and told Buster to sit in a seat at the front window so she could find him right away. At the appointed hour she drove past the window and saw him sitting alone in the restaurant. Obviously, she did not show. Instead she wrote him again, telling him she was just too shy and nervous to keep their date.

Jeanie made subsequent dates, not showing up and giving Buster excuses. His letters to her post office box showed a desperate man willing to do anything to meet her. She wrote him a final letter telling him it could never be, which thoroughly broke his heart. He never knew it was his ex-wife.

Now, while Jeanie got to put her ex through some grief what did this get her? Possibly, a great story for her friends (especially girlfriends.) Some brief satisfaction. But it also means that during that time she was putting considerable effort and attention towards her ex. Would it have been better if she spent that time and energy meeting new people, gaining positive experiences, etc.?

Chapter 16
Getting Your Head Straight

"Reject your sense of injury and the injury itself disappears." Marcus Aurelius

I put that last story in for your amusement. However, if you truly are thinking a lot about your ex and his girlfriend with anger and revenge in mind, you may be having trouble getting your head straight.

In my case, the element of surprise made it worse. My surprise of "How could you be unfaithful to me?" was followed by the greater surprise of "How could you go into partnership with someone else without telling me when we have been partners for 20 years?" And the surprise of "How could you leave me?" was replaced by "How could you leave me with no income?" And then the surprise of "How could you ask to have my air points so you can get her a seat in first class?" led to the ultimate surprise of "How can you ask to come back and stay with me temporarily so you can have an operation?"

One surprise after another cascading down like boulders on a mountainside until I finally "got it" that I had been living in an illusion. I just did not matter anymore.

In the book *Divorce Hangover*, Anne Walther[32] writes about what I would call objectifying the situation. You are grieving, angry, etc., because you have suffered a great loss. Anger, bitterness, and grief during divorce are all about the loss you have suffered as a result of the breakup—not about the other people. Your anger may be focused on your ex or on your ex's new lover or even on yourself, but that is not what you are actually upset about. You are upset about loss; loss of something that typically is replaceable, although not always.

Consider this: if you lost your spouse but immediately had a lover or spouse much more wonderful than the last, if you suddenly had more money than before, a better house, if your children were with you and happy, would you be as upset with your spouse or his lover? No, you would not, even though that person caused you to go through a divorce. Why? Because it is the loss that has you so upset.

You have lost ground in your life, lost your house, lost income, lost friends you shared, lost your lover, your partner, lost companionship, lost a parent to help raise your children and maybe lost the ability to trust. So it is not the people you are grieving over, it is the losses. It's important to make that distinction; it will help you adjust. It will help you know where your time and energy must now go, which is not in the direction of anger, revenge and obsession but in the direction of filling your life back up with what and who you need.

If you can understand that it is the loss not the person you are upset about you can depersonalize those feelings. Anger can be a protective device to keep you from looking at the loss you have suffered. That loss may be very hard to accept. But if you can realize this, it will allow you to set aside your anger and live in a more positive way. *You have to choose being happy over being right.*

You do have control of what emotions you will focus on each day. You can decide to either get "justice" and "control" by making your ex's life miserable or you can choose to be happy on this day. Choose to move toward a more positive place, a more productive lifestyle. As long as your focus is on rectifying the injustice of your situation, regaining control over your spouse, or sinking further into depression you will not be able to make your inner or outer life better.

Depression can be anger turned inward. You may be angry with yourself for playing the fool or for loving in the first place. You can't control what people do to you but you can control how you react. Choose actions and thoughts that pull you into the light, actions and thoughts that can bring you closer to happiness again. Move toward the positive and away from the negative.

You may argue "but then I am letting him get away with it," or "I can't take this lying down." The truth is, your happiness is more important than you making a point, being right or applying justice—and you can't be happy if you are on this kind of pointless mission.

Take time to objectify that loss. Write it out. For example, "I have lost: my lover, my partner for life, my job (as a wife or husband), half my assets, income, money to raise the children properly, my home, my self- esteem, my advisor, my companion, my best friend, my dog, custody of the children, control over their care, etc. The list in a divorce can be mighty and huge and seem utterly overwhelming, but write it down.

Anne Walther says that the emotional tailspin of a divorce is fueled by feelings of anger, depression, confusion and loss of control. The key to pulling out of a tailspin is moving from emotional to rational. This is not to say you should deny the stages of grief a divorce entails. To get to rational, you will have to go through the stages of grief as described by Elizabeth-Ross in the classic book *On Death and Dying*. You cannot avoid this, whether you are the one leaving or the one being left. Allow yourself to stop and take a look at what happened. Which of the states below are you in? It is OK to be in any of them just don't get stuck there.

- Denial: You may be in denial trying to pretend it's not happening or pretending it's not so bad.

- Anger: Or you may be in a state of perpetual anger over what you have lost; anger and disappointment in others.

- Bargaining: Perhaps trying to work things out with your soon-to-be ex or bargaining with God that if he will give you a pass this time, you will do better.

- Depression: Inevitably follows, sucking you down into its gray maw. Allow yourself to wallow in this a bit.

- Acceptance: Finally, come to acceptance. This is not lying down and taking it, not letting others trample over you—it's just accepting where you are and what has happened so you can move on to a better place. This is what you have lost; this is where you are at. It is what it is. Having an awareness of these stages will help you pass through to a place where you can be rational once again.

Think and Act, Not Feel and React

Feel and react is what we do instinctively. Like a wasp trapped in a house, we can continue butting our heads against a window. Or we can choose to stop, look around, and assess the situation. Using your brain is the best defense in a crisis.

Scream, yell, cry, allow those emotions to be there and get it all out. Write down what you have lost. But then, objectify the situation. Like the men in Mission Control at NASA, think strategically about what you can do, should do next. After you have thoroughly examined your feelings, put them in a box where you can take them out and look at them now and then.

Then, with your feelings under control, you will be able to think and act, not feel and react.

Everyone from attorneys to investigators to counselors agree that your most important action now for your own sake and your children's is to think and act rationally not emotionally. Part of what will help you get to that rational place is examining some of the underlying questions running around in your head.

Anne Walther believes that divorce becomes like a hangover—the leftover negative feelings clouding your every day, affecting your choices and decisions—and that we must get over that hangover so we can go on with our lives, moving in a positive direction for our own sake and that of our children.

Chapter 17
Was the Divorce Inevitable?

"We cannot change our past. We cannot change the fact that people act in a certain way. We cannot change the inevitable. The only thing we can do is play on the one string we have, and that is our attitude."
Charles R. Swindoll

Was the divorce inevitable? What caused the divorce? Did either of you have unrealistic expectations when you got married? Did you expect him to change?

When I look at my own marriage, I know that divorce may have been inevitable. When I married my husband, I knew he had previously been in an "open" marriage because he believed he could not and did not want to be monogamous. In fact, we broke up over this very issue when dating.

Finally he had said, "I know I can do this. I am more mature now. I want to be in a monogamous relationship for the rest of my life." After we were married for awhile I thought this would be the case. But somewhere after that seven year (itch) time period, I saw how excited he was by certain women. I saw his attention to me go out the window when an attractive woman was near.

We hired a secretary who was cute and sweet and young. I saw his feelings for her develop. When I returned from a trip out of town, he announced that she had quit suddenly. I had gotten close to her too and was astonished. He explained that she had feelings for him, that she needed his consolation due to her marriage problems, and that she had quit because of this.

I knew that she was not interested in him. I knew there was more. He finally confessed that he had kissed her when he walked her to her car one evening. She had left because of his inappropriate attentions. At that time, I left him and went away for two weeks to think about this, about the meaning of it.

He begged forgiveness. He swore he would never, ever allow that to happen again. He said, "You pick the secretaries. We will only hire, unattractive, older women!" He had been a wonderful husband in all other respects.

I did not want to give the marriage up. But I knew in my heart of hearts, I would always have to be on guard.

And so our marriage, good in all other respects, continued for another 13 years. Had I been smarter, I would have left him then. That experience and what I knew of his former life was enough information that had I been thinking rationally and not emotionally, I might have left him then. A younger me would have been able to build a new relationship with someone else; a different, more faithful character.

Looking back, I can see that the signs were there for things to happen the way they did. The divorce was inevitable. It just took time and the right set of circumstances to fall apart. In my life, I had felt that having gone 20 years, and those years being good years and our relationship being strong sexually and emotionally, I believed we would be together for the rest of our lives.

Individuals with addictions, whether it be alcohol, drugs, sex or gambling, cannot be stopped by your love. Individuals with bad habits like infidelity, anger, abuse, continual financial problems or habitual unemployment will not be changed by your love. Marriages with these problems may be doomed.

So, knowing that the divorce was inevitable helps. The idea here is to stop the "What if I had..." or the shoulda, woulda, coulda agonies we put ourselves through. Stopping those repetitious thoughts with rational thinking allows your mind to move on to more productive places.

Replace "what if" with "I did the best I could at the time" and "my job is to now play the hand of cards I have been dealt to the best of my ability."

Getting Over It...Letting Go at Last

The longer your marriage or your relationship lasted, the longer it may take you to get over it. If you find yourself trying to leave the door open for that lost love, if you find excuses to contact or call him or her, if you want to delay the divorce, you may be having a hard time letting go.

Counselors say you can't really be open to a new love relationship while you have one foot in the old one. Worse, you may be comparing any new man in your life to the best qualities of the old love (forgetting about all his shortcomings) so that no one can ever compare or exceed your ex.

"Magical thinking" refers to beliefs not supported by reality, but things we want to believe on an emotional level. Magical thinking may be hiding in the back of your brain conjuring up a fantasy wherein your lover comes to his senses, realizes what a tragic mistake he has made and comes crawling back on his knees. It may lead you to think that all it will take is time for him to see that that other woman is really all about. It may make you think that "true love" never really dies and that you will be reunited in the future. Or you may fantasize that your lover will become seriously ill or injured and call for you to come to his side and save him.

This is fairy tale thinking and it gets women in deep, sticky trouble. It is doubly destructive as it ties up your emotions, stops you from growing and keeps you out of new relationships.

Counselors say that holding on like this is the result of not fully expressing your feelings of grief, anger, rage or fear, trying to deny or suppress them. Their advice is to ask the question, "If I let go of this person—if I wipe him out of my life completely—what is the worst that can happen?"

The answer may be that you would have to face being alone, perhaps alone for always. The anchorage you felt with that person in your life would be gone. Or you might be afraid that you would have to go out and start the scary, difficult world of dating again. Worst of all, if the relationship were completely over, if you knew you would never, ever, speak to that person again or see them again, you might have to take a serious look at what caused the relationship to end. You might be afraid deep down that you were the problem.

Try writing the answer to that question on a piece of paper. "If it is all over, if that person is out of my life forever, what would that feel like? What is the worst that would happen? Why do I want that connection still?" Your answers should come from deep down, from your subconscious. Information coming from the purely emotional side of you written down in cold print may show you how illogical your thinking is. Love has little to do with logic but if you can get these feelings out into the light of day, logic may have a chance to overcome them.

After you have taken as hard a look at this as you can; make a conscious decision to move in new directions. The more support networks you have the better. A job, coworkers you like, friends, family members who understand and care, a church, other social groups or clubs where you feel an affiliation to other members are helpful. Fulfillment in your work, whether that be professional or personal, is very helpful here. Now you can go through your life and eliminate reminders of that other person you loved and lost (and may still love.)

Cleaning House

Dr. Bruce Fisher in his book *Rebuilding*[33] suggests the following actions to help you move on in your life:

1. Go through your house and remove all of those things that tend to keep you thinking about your former love partner. Pictures, gifts, and similar mementos can be removed so that they are not a constant reminder.

2. If you lived together then you may need to rearrange the furniture in the house, perhaps even to make the house look as different as possible from the way it was when you were living together.

3. The shared bed is often an especially important symbol. You may need to put the bed in another room, sell it, or at least move it to a new spot in the bedroom. Change the coverings for a new look.

4. Make a collection of all those reminders of your former love relationship and store them in a box in the attic, garage, or basement.

5. Some weekend you may choose to do some implosive grieving, whereby you bring out all of these mementos and set aside a period of time to grieve a heavily as possible. This period will probably be very depressing and having another person around for support could help. Becoming as much out of control as possible in your grieving may help you to let go more rapidly. By increasing the intensity of the grief, this implosive grieving may shorten the number of weeks or months it takes you to let go fully.

6. Refuse to play the game. Don't return phone calls, letters, or emails from the person you are trying to let go of. You will have to become assertive, or perhaps even start hanging up the phone or returning letters unanswered and unopened.

7. Whenever you find yourself weeping about that person, think about something painful or something unpleasant in the love relationship. That will lead you to stop thinking about the person. Choose another image to concentrate on, instead of focusing on the past love.

Being aware of how many other women—nice, beautiful, smart, successful women—have gone through the same thing will help you to separate yourself from the event. Listing your spouse's faults, listing the times he has hurt you or let you down or pretending that this event happened a long time ago will all make you feel remote from the event. In a year you will find some relief in looking back and seeing who he really is.

Recovery from divorce is similar to the stages of grieving. As time goes on, the distance from this event will give you a different, more accurate perspective on life. You will form a new identity, stronger and more independent. Trust me, it will happen.

Chapter 18
Emotional Recovery Begins

I was certainly not in the mentally rational place described above. I was mired part-time in grieving and part-time in despair and could not seem to get out of it. At this time in my life, several people came forth to help me.

Susan, my friend who had been through three divorces herself, was there for me almost every day, spending hours advising, commiserating and helping. It was her house I went to when I was at my worst.

My wonderful daughter-in-law, Mary, called me every day, "just checking in with you." That meant so much. She had several of my friends write letters to me telling me how much they loved me and gave me a quilt that represented hope and healing to her and to me. My sons, who loved my husband as though he had been their real father, grieved for themselves and for me.

I called my old friend Gene who had known both my husband and me. He was shocked. I bemoaned my age. He said, "Listen honey, 60 is the new 40. Haven't you heard?" For some reason this saying cheered me immeasurably. He was right. I did not feel 60. I felt like 40 and could do as much if not more than I had done at that age. I put on this new perspective and went forward.

If you know someone who is going through a divorce, particularly if they have been dumped, reach out to them. I had a small group of girlfriends who I had met with monthly for more than 20 years. They recoiled when I told them Rob had left. Only one of them—who was also single—called to see if I was OK after that and invited me out. The others (all married) acted as though divorce were contagious.

A neighbor I did not know that well came to me and gave me a big bear hug. Things like that meant the world. An old friend I had not seen in ages took me out to lunch. A woman I knew from the YMCA sauna enveloped me in her life when I told her. She insisted I go to Zumba classes with her. I never would have done this on my own and it wound up changing my life.

Divorce Recovery Programs

At the suggestion of a friend who is a psychologist, I reluctantly went to a Divorce Recovery Program run by a local church. On the first night, as I went in, I said to myself, "I will probably not stay. It is probably a religious thing." I walked into the auditorium and to my amazement there were more than 150 people there. They broke us into small groups of six to eight, and assigned two leaders to each group.

On the first night we met, each person in the group had to tell his or her story. I was one month out of my husband's leaving and still in shock. Still, I thought I would tell my story objectively, that there would be no histrionics from me.

Some people spoke solemnly, some cried; some cried a lot. But none cried more than me. As I started to tell my story, I heard myself say, "He left me. He left me for someone else." Hearing my own voice say this, I began to cry, first in small sighs, then in great gasping sobs. I could not continue. I pulled back and covered my face with my hands. The moderator soothed me.

I looked around and saw that most of the people in my group were women—good looking women, women who seemed nice and smart, women who should not have been left. I felt so much better hearing their stories. My sorrow turned to anger on their behalf. For the most part, their stories were similar to mine. Their husbands had left to start a new life with someone younger, someone who made him feel good. So much for loyalty.

Find One or Start One

Divorce recovery programs are so important to a person going through divorce that I would like to explain their benefits and describe how to start one.

"Divorce is messy." This understatement by Ralph Starling, who founded and directs The Divorce Recovery Program of the First Baptist Church in Richmond VA, is one of the reasons that most churches do not try to create their own divorce recovery programs. I was fortunate to have this one available to me in my city. If there is not one in your area, read how the Richmond program was begun and consider starting your own.

Ralph Starling was a minister in Marin, Calif. During his first year at that church, he noticed one woman who came to services each Sunday but stayed in the back of the church and cried. Members of the congregation told him her name was Sherry and that she was recently divorced.

Mr. Starling said, "We did not know what to do for her, but she taught us what to do. She opened her home to others in the congregation who were newly divorced or separated. She provided a safe haven for people to share feelings and support. The numbers of people who came to her home each weekend rapidly multiplied. It was clear there was a widespread need for this type of program."

Sherry's informal gatherings created the basis of what became a formal divorce recovery program. The success of this program, led by Mr. Starling, led the First Baptist Church to offer him the opportunity to come to Richmond, Va., to run their program. Once they did, their program exploded.

The basic structure of this program is intense. Yours, of course, can be a simpler, less formal model. I am presenting here the full schedule for those who may want to create a complete program.

On Sunday nights, all participants listen to a presentation by a speaker on the topic of separation and divorce. This is followed by a "testimonial" from a former program participant telling his story of personal pain and growth.

Then small groups are formed. These small groups stay together for an eight-week program. They follow a set format of sharing their stories, insights and problems and are led by two facilitators who are former participants themselves. While deep and lasting friendships can develop during the small group interaction, participants are not allowed to begin a romantic relationship with one another during the eight-week program. In addition, there are social events and retreats especially designed to get people through the holidays.

After you finish the initial eight-week program, there is a second ongoing program about rebuilding called the First Step Workshop. Held on Friday nights, the First Step program addresses the issues that cause marriages to fail.

Geri Hale-Cooper, coordinator of the 50 volunteers who run the Richmond program and a former program participant, advises that before you become involved with someone else, invest in yourself. Try to analyze what went wrong and make changes before you are locked into a new relationship. Feeling better in a new relationship is not the same as being better. You still have the same baggage. After the grieving, it is time to look at issues that may have caused the marriage to fail.

Gerri said, "I went through the program myself. I had left my marriage. I was consumed by feelings of failure." Gerri was so good at helping others that Ralph Starling asked her to make a three-year commitment to manage the volunteer program.

That was 15 years ago. She said, "I found at this group a community, a place to express and share my feelings. They understood me. I felt I had something to offer to others. I began to help with the program. I got through my own crisis by helping others."

She added, "We are trained to handle different situations. We see people here who are very angry and very sad. We get people who are on the verge of suicide. We call everyone in this program during the week and ask them how they are feeling. On occasion, we have even accompanied them to the hospital."

Ralph Starling said, "I cannot tell you how often I hear, 'This program has literally saved my life.' "

Viviane, a recent participant who decided to become a facilitator herself said about the group experience, "I don't think I would have made it without this group. My group was like the island of misfit toys, all of us were missing a piece but together we were whole. I want to give back to others what was given to me."

Heather is a young mother of a six year old. She and her husband had separated once before. They were back together again and she felt they were making progress. "But one day, he just said, 'That's it.' He left us. I was in shock. When my counselor suggested the program, I thought I would go check it out but did not know if I would stay. When I saw all those people there, I was amazed. The first night, in our small group, they went around the room and I couldn't bear to tell my story. But then I felt so welcomed. It became a place of healing for me. The boundaries session was particularly helpful. I learned that I respected other people's boundaries but never my own. It was eye-opening. Every speaker truly had something to add."

What Makes A Program Successful?

Leadership: Participants and volunteers say that Ralph Starling's leadership and focus has enabled the program to be truly viable and effective for participants. They, in turn, are so grateful they want to give back to others.

The Use of Peer Groups: Peer groups have been successful therapies for alcohol and drug addiction, weight control and other conditions—some would argue more successful than individual counseling.

Volunteers: The strength of the program is its utilization of volunteers. Many, such as Gerri and Robin Hale Cooper, have continued as volunteers for years. The only paid position is that of the director, and the rest of the program relies on approximately 50 unpaid volunteers. One paid position provides services for 200 people over an eight-week period every year.

If there are no formal divorce recovery programs in your area, you can start your own. It can be big or small and as in-depth and ongoing as you want it to be. Here are some tips on how help other participants.

1. Be a good listener. This validates their feelings. Show you understand how much pain they are in.

2. Focus on the person's feelings, not the facts and not the other person. Ask them, "How does that make you feel?"

3. Answer a question with a question. If they ask, "What should I do?" Respond with, "What are your options?"

4. Resist the impulse to give advice. Advice can be invalidating. It can lead the person to feel she ought to do something she really doesn't want to do. Instead, reinforce the person's decision making abilities. "I know you can make the right choice." Let them explore options, seeing how they feel about each one.

5. Avoid platitudes that minimize the pain of the situation such as, "just forget about him" or "you are better off without him." [34]

Part VII
Change

Chapter 19
A New Life

"Nobody can go back and start a new beginning, but anyone can start today and make a new ending." Maria Robinson

Networking

As I said before, networking is crucial to building a new life. Any social networks you create, whether through work, church, your children's activities, neighborhood associations, clubs, meet- up groups, local chambers of commerce, mastermind groups, courses you are taking—any of these can lead to new jobs, new friends for you and your children, answers to questions you have and ways to solve problems.

I had become a freelance writer and was working alone in my home. I needed to connect with other people who were running their own businesses. I joined a national group called Ladies Who Launch, a sort of incubator program for new business owners or wannabe business owners.

I spent six weeks in the group, meeting six women and the facilitator, Suzy Galvez. They were all business women, women with a head on their shoulders, women who were ambitious and interested in growth. I loved it. They loved hearing my marketing ideas and I felt smart again. Together, with Suzy's guidance, we each formulated a plan to achieve our entrepreneurial goals.

There is also an organization called the National Speakers Association. I had attended it with my husband for years and always loved it for the inspiration it gave me. The membership costs are steep but one of the Ladies Who Launch members enabled me to go to the NSA conference that year.

During an evening event there, I met a woman who runs a dating boot camp in New York. Diana Kirschner, author of *Love in Ninety Days*. Hearing my story, she enveloped me. "Honey, dye your hair darker, get a push-up bra, lose those glasses and you'll do fine. You've got a great figure and a cute face."

When we have a path we can do almost anything. Diana inspired me and gave me hope. She told me, "I want you to go around this club and introduce yourself to three men. Do it now." I did and one of them, a professor from Arizona, sat with me during dinner.

I went home, bought her great book, did get a better bra and dyed my hair a shade darker. At social functions I took my glasses off, which meant I often failed to recognize people and occasionally ate things without knowing what they were but hey, those are minor problems.

Makeover

I decided to take my makeover a few steps further, but not just for the men that might come into my life. These steps were for me. Being pleased with your body and face are self-esteem builders that make you feel better every day.

I had begun to see my mother in the mirror. Sagging happens, not just your breasts, tummy and butt, but your face. I knew two women doctors who frequented the sauna at the YMCA. I asked them about plastic surgery. One said to me, "If you do it, get the best." The other said, "One of the Top 10 in the country is in Virginia Beach, two hours from here."

So I called Dr. James Carraway[35] and scheduled a consult.

Dr. Carraway is a tall, thin, Irish looking man who acts with the assurance of someone who is an accomplished artist in his field. Sitting in his waiting room, I watched other women, beautiful women, come and go, some from as far as Europe.

After taking photographs, and studying my face from different angles, he said, "I can take 10 years off your appearance." That was more than I had hoped for. I spoke with his nurse who gave me the price of the full face lift, throat lift, forehead lift and eye lift. I gulped and prayed my 95 Toyota would last another 150,000 miles.

Dr. Carraway explained that during surgery, he would take a small amount of fat from my thigh (I have plenty to spare) and freeze it to use it as a "filler" for places in my face that needed filling out. He asked me to stay on a healthy, green vegetable-rich, lean protein diet with no smoking, no alcohol, starting three months ahead of surgery.

The day of the surgery, the doctor went over everything with me, then started the anesthesia. I remember nothing after that but the doctor assured me later that I was "awake" and responsive but felt no discomfort. Following the surgery, the biggest surprise was the lack of pain, a pulling sensation yes, but no pain.

Looking in the mirror was pretty scary—bruises, stitches, black eyes— but I could see a different face emerging. I was told stay down, no bending, no lifting, not even a heavy purse on my shoulder and I must sleep on my back with my head elevated for a week. The face at this stage is like a cake just taken from the oven, done but not quite set. Staying quiet was the hardest part.

By day four I could see that I had a new face. It looked much improved. Weeks later, without the bruises, I saw my aunt. I did not tell her I had surgery. She squinted at me and said, "You look different." I asked, "Better or worse?" She replied, "Better…much, much better!"

In talking with professionals about plastic surgery, many say you must want to do it for yourself. Many women come to plastic surgeons following a divorce because they want to be remade into a new, raving beauty. You can be substantially improved but not recreated by plastic surgery.

And the best plastic surgeries are enhancements of the person's own natural look, not a radically different look. There is a certain symmetry to everyone's face and body; you do not want to lose that symmetry by putting a nose or eye shape that does not really go with the rest of you. A very good surgeon, like Dr. Carraway, will know how to work with you so all your parts go together and it all looks natural.

Alternatives to Cosmetic Surgery

In case you don't want to take that radical a step, there are numerous new procedures now available as a substitute for surgery. A local spa owner shared the following with me: "You lose one percent of your collagen every year after 30. Collagen loss contributes to the sagging that later requires cosmetic surgery. Exposure to sun and toxins in the environment increases that rate but can be slowed by care."

Skin tightening with laser is an alternative to a face lift. The laser acts by heating the dermis to make it contract. Thermage is similar but uses radio waves instead of light. The spa owner continued, "Thermage is a one-time only treatment and the success rate for thermage is less than 60 percent. It is painful. We don't do that here." With both procedures the anesthesia is topical and it takes six months to see the results.

In lieu of surgery, there are also solutions that can be injected or used as a complement, such as fillers like Restylane, Juvederm or collagen. You might try a dermal filler to see how a more permanent surgical procedure would look. These fillers can last anywhere from six months to five years. Some physicians favor real fat injections as they have found that your own fat (taken from your thighs) can actually grow, merging with your own tissue.

Dance

Back at the YMCA, my friend Kim made me go to Zumba classes. I have a hard time with anything that requires coordination and have dropped many aerobics classes that required some sense of kinesthetics. So, I was reluctant. The instructor Joella said, "Do whatever you want. This is about feeling good. No one is watching your butt; they are all worried about theirs." And it was true.

Once I heard the music—Latin, Salsa, Meringue and a little hip hop thrown in—it had me. I came to every class. The Latin music, I found, did something great to my endorphins. The only time I was not depressed was when I danced to this music. I found a Latin music channel on cable and played it at home—all the time. I became obsessed. After six months I managed to get many of the steps right. Then I really got brave.

Someone at the YMCA mentioned dances that were open to the public. I decided to go to one of these. I went by myself with lots of fear in my heart. I had not been to a dance like this since high school. I walked into the hall. There were two women sitting alone at a table. I asked if I could join them. They were friendly and welcomed me. It was an older crowd, my age and older. Good old rock and roll was being blasted out by an equally old (and good) band.

After a few songs, to my complete astonishment, men began to ask me to dance. I have always been what Helen Gurley Brown, editor of *Cosmopolitan* magazine and author of the famous classic *Sex and the Single Girl*, called a "mouse." I am not used to garnering attention at parties or dances. Was it that I was the new girl in town? Was it that (as I secretly believed) I looked younger than the other women there?

I had not felt attractive since my husband left. This was my big breakthrough. Men were literally waiting to dance with me. Wow, how fun. Here was a completely unexpected turn of events.

Then some strange synergy happened. At the YMCA, where I had been a member for many years with no attention paid to me whatsoever by the opposite sex, I suddenly began to get attention from men. Some I was attracted to, others not, but yes, men began to make advances. It had now been two years since my husband and I had separated and I was finally beginning to date for the first time in 20 years.

Chapter 20
Back in the Dating Pool

"Sometimes I get tired. Sometimes I get bored. And sometimes all I want, more than anything else in the world, is to go on a freaking date."
Kiersten White

So you won't think that a handsome prince swept into my life and fulfilled my romantic dreams I want you to know about some of the characters I dated or almost dated during this time.

There was "Big John," who I actually never dated but did dance with. He was from the Y and had plenty of opportunities to ask me on a real date but did not. He is the one who told me about some local dances. He danced with me there many times but it was not until another man there began to date me steadily that he began to ask me out. It was always a casual, "Well, I'll take you there if you want to go" or "Let's have lunch." By that time I was already involved with someone else.

Another man at the Y began to chat with me about photography. He asked me to meet him at a local book store and café to continue our discussion. We sat and talked for an hour. No mention was made of getting anything to eat or drink. I was thirsty after so much talk and finally said, "I am going to get some tea. He leaned back in his chair and grinned arrogantly and said, "Buy me a cup of coffee while you are up." My mouth dropped open but I bought him a cup.

He saw the expression on my face and asked about it. I said, "Well usually, the men I go out with offer to buy me drinks." He said he thought I "owed him" after all the useful advice he had been giving me. I figured he felt I owed him even more than the coffee. He wanted to see me again after that and I declined. I wondered if I was out of touch with dating customs?

I interviewed another man for a magazine article. He knew a great deal about the history of our city and was glad to share it with me. Because he was there at my request, sharing his time and knowledge, I bought lunch for both of us.

He asked me out several times after that. On our first date at a local pub we listened to music. He bought nothing for himself and nothing for me. On our second date he met me and some friends who were sharing pizza. He ate nothing, asked for nothing and paid for nothing.

On our third date, we met at a restaurant and were supposed to go hiking afterwards. Again, he ordered nothing and drank nothing. I was starving and ordered lunch for myself. He never offered to pay and so I paid for it myself. I asked him directly if he had financial problems. He said no, he just wasn't hungry. I pressed it and noted he never ordered anything, not even coffee. He still would not open up. After that, confused and wondering how we could ever have a dating relationship, I declined further dates.

There is more. There was Tom, who wrote beautifully and was a delightful companion but only asked me out on Thursdays. At first I thought he was spending each weekend with his teenage daughter. But then he confessed that, thanks to internet dating, he was seeing a different woman each night. My night happened to be Thursday. At least I was not Monday.

My new dating persona received two marriage proposals in one year, both from older men, neither of which I accepted. There is a lot of angst, futile first starts and rejection on the path to finding someone.

I did find a man who is a wonderful lover, great dancer and willing to go anywhere and do anything, who also adores me and would like to get married. However, he has elements in his history that give me pause and I am too gun-shy at this time to move closer to him.

So, it is not a perfect world and the older you get, the less market there is and the less marketable you become. I would say from my vantage point, do not put up with any unpleasant stuff. You know now that you can survive alone. That is a hard-won piece of information. Cherish it.

My conclusions after these experiences were that older men tend to be more romantic and generous. I met many new people. I found that men who were widowers seem to like and trust women and are eager to get married again. Divorced men, on the other hand, are wary, suspicious and often have a bit of residual bitterness towards the female sex.

Chapter 21
What do you Need a Man for Anyway?

"Sometimes you need to stand alone to prove you can still stand." Anonymous

Being mammals, we all need others of our species to help us get through life. Codependency has been given a bad connotation in our language. The reality is we are all codependent. However, we can choose who to be codependent with.

Today's lifestyles are more individual than in any other time in history. Just as infidelity and divorce have become more acceptable, it is also socially acceptable (pretty much anyway) to choose to live with your parents, with your kids, with your best girlfriend, with your gay guy friend, with your lover (either sex), with tenants in your house or to live alone.

But, if you are desperate for a man, stop and take a look at your reasons:

1) **Loneliness**: Loneliness is simply a type of pain. It can be endured. It can also be cured; cured with new friends, cured with volunteering, cured with animals or taking care of children, cured with old relationships reestablished, cured with family. Is there something you have always been interested in? You can find a club or group or you can create one. Be determined that you can and will survive this and be happy again. If it is loneliness driving you, try bringing new friends into your circle; consider taking in a tenant or sharing someone else's home to get you through that initial shock of being alone. This is a transition period. You may have lost someone that to you was the center of your life. If you work through this period for, say at least a year, you will feel an incredible strength building in you. That strength comes from knowing you are making it—you, all by

yourself. It may result in you having more confidence than you have ever had before. If you do this, once you are in a new relationship, you will show an inner confidence. The knowledge that you don't have to settle for any kind of bad behavior will be internalized. I know many divorced women who have decided to forgo the dating scene and are happily living alone or with friends or relatives.

2) **Hurt:** Is it because you've been stung and need to prove (to yourself or others) that you are desirable? Is it your fantasy to make your ex jealous? If you are desperate, it will show and you are in the perfect position to make a really bad choice for your next mate. You may be on the verge of getting in deep with someone even worse than your ex and en route to your next divorce.

3) **Ego**: Let's hope your ego has something to depend upon other than men. There is so much more to you than that. Your new identity can be built on a solid foundation of self-acceptance and love. It can be attached to your career, your role in your church and other social groups, your role as a parent, or to the special skills and talents you have and by how much you mean to the people in your life. It used to be that being unmarried was almost as bad as wearing the scarlet letter through life. That is not true anymore. You don't have to feel like a spinster aunt or a failure in life because you are not married. Look at all the very smart and extremely successful women of the world (Martha Stewart, Oprah Winfrey, Dr. Condoleezza Rice, and Maureen Dowd to name a few) who are deliberately choosing not to get married. They get the companionship they need without marriage.

4) **As an escort**: He probably never wanted to go where you did anyway so why not find a stable of girlfriends/guyfriends and gayfriends who like the same things you do. Yes, I know you will feel awkward with your friends who are couples. But, if they love you they will continue to invite you and you simply ask if you can bring a friend of your choice.

5) **Sex**: That's a good reason, although sex, as you know, can really, really mess up your life. It can also be dangerous to your health if you are not careful. By all means, if you start dating you must insist your man uses protection. If he doesn't want to then he has not been using it with other women and who knows where he has been or what diseases he may have. When you start dating it is perfectly acceptable practice these days to ask your man to have a STD (sexually transmitted disease) test done before you consummate your relationship or at least use a condom. This will show him that you are particular about who you sleep with. He will respect you for it. Don't put your life at risk in an effort to be polite. An alternative is to have sex by yourself. There are plenty of women, nice women, who use vibrators and are quite content with that. A simple $24.95 device does not require that you get plastic surgery, dye your hair, lose 15 pounds or wear heels that are excruciating painful. It also will never compare you unfavorably to a young neighbor in a bikini.

6) **Love**: An even better reason. You believe in love. You know that the love of your life is out there somewhere. That may be true. It may also be true that you will expend your time, energy, self-esteem and focus looking for someone who is not there. If this is your dream…well, it's your life and if that is your dream, by all means, follow it. But do it in a fun way, a light way, so that if, at the end of your search, you wind up with some kissed frogs, a broken heart from lost loves, rejections and nothing more, you will at least be able to say you had fun while looking. As Sally Warren[36] said, "There may not be another lover/husband/soulmate in your life for a long time, perhaps never again…so it is better to say that out loud now and be prepared."

Women Who Did Not Marry

"Every woman who agrees to this ideology of oneness will spend her life as someone else's person, not as her own. She will never quite know who she is. The trappings of oneness have built into them frustration, dependency, disappointment and a ceaseless need for approval from 'the one.'" Sonya Freidman, *Men Are Just Deserts*

My friend Sarah, one of the sweetest and most loving women I know, went through three marriages. Each time, she was betrayed by an unfaithful man she loved. After the last experience, she determined she would give up the dating game for good.

Now her life is full in a different way. She misses dating and loving but she has no anxiety, no one to try to appease or please. Her focus, her time, her energy are hers to use as she wishes. Her many friends, her family, her interest in alternative medicine fill her life with purpose and companionship. She has clarity, focus and peace and that, she feels, is enough.

I believe in love. I believe in marriage. I believe you can be very happy in a marriage. But I now know that there are also benefits to believing you can leave a situation whenever you want. Give yourself the gift of growing strong on your own. You will always be grateful you did.

The following highly successful women opted not to marry: Jane Austen, author of *Pride and Prejudice*; Emily Bronte, author of *Wuthering Heights*; Jane Addams, who received a Nobel Peace Prize for her work as advocate of poor women and children; Oprah Winfrey, who said "Now I realize why I did not marry, why I do not have children...I was meant to care for these children (in Africa)"; Emily Dickenson, the most famous American female poet; Jodie Foster, winner of two Oscars, director and actress; Clarissa Howe Barton, battlefield heroine who founded the American Red Cross; Ellen Glasgow, Pulitzer Prize winning author; Rachel Carson, author of *Silent Spring* who founded the American environmental movement; Florence Nightingale, the nurse who changed the way medicine was delivered on the battlefield; and Louisa May Alcott, author of *Little Women*—to name just a few.

Chapter 22
If You Must Have a Man

"Love is a fruit in season at all times and within reach of every hand."
Mother Teresa

So, despite what we have said about needing a man, despite the odds of him cheating, despite the possibility of having to experience the horrors of a divorce again, despite all this, if you decide you must have a man in your life, read on.

The best books I have found on love are these three, all of which have been heavily quoted in this book: *Act like a Lady, Think like a Man*[37] by Steve Harvey, *The Secret Psychology* of *How We Fall in Love*[38] by Dr. Paul Dobransky and *Love in Ninety Days*[39] by Dr. Diana Kirschner.

Love in Ninety Days gives you a path to gear yourself up for the dating scene. Dr. Diana Kirschner has a concrete, step-by-step, "boot camp" plan that has worked for hundreds of her readers in her book. She focuses on building self-esteem, a necessary ingredient in the dating game. She writes, "I would say that if you have the courage, the time and the determination to make 'love' your primary goal, this blueprint should get you there."

The book helps you do inner work (self-esteem, stopping self-sabotage, building confidence) and the outer work (your appearance, beauty, clothes.) The book addresses some of the negative patterns you can develop while dating. She suggests you make a real quest of this, utilizing a dating diary, finding a dating mentor who can help you stay on track and taking action steps to reach your goal. Dr. Kirschner's attitude is that "Now is the right time to believe in love."

Act Like a Lady, Think Like a Man is the honest and invaluable perspective of a man (Steve Harvey) who tells it like he sees it. Harvey's advice centers on a woman having standards and holding men to those standards. His definition of a man who could be a serious contender for your hand is that he must be a man who can show you he wants to protect you, provide for you and profess his feelings for you. He writes that women must demand fidelity and be absolutely willing to walk if they do not get it.

If you really want to comprehend the way that men fall in love, read *The Secret Psychology of How We Fall in Love*. The importance and value of going through the ancient process of male-female dynamics in courtship is explained. This is a serious read but the author shows a unique picture of what must happen in a relationship in order for a man to fall in love and stay in love. It is by far the best book I have ever found on this complex subject.

Too Picky?

One more thought on dating…You may have noticed that the number of available men is far fewer than the number of available women in the same age group. Men are besieged with female admirers. That does not mean you should not try—you should put on your competitive hat and get out there.

You may have also noticed that these men are not quite the same adorable hunks that were out there the last time you dated. They may have little, or no hair on their heads, they may have one or two medical problems. They are most likely, if over 50, hard of hearing. They may not be able to dance for three hours at a time. They may have age-related crankiness and fatigue.

But if their souls are good, if you can trust your heart and your pocketbook with them, that is saying a lot. My girlfriend's father lost his wife to a blood clot. He grieved and tried to find someone as wonderful as she was. He waited years for one special woman he was taken with to stop rebuffing him but she never did. He gave up many opportunities with lovely women who cherished him. They were just not as attractive as his ideal. He now has Parkinson's disease and is alone. He said to me "I wish I had not been so picky."

Going on the Net

One of the most amazing consequences of the computer age is the internet dating game. It is now not only possible but also convenient to meet dozens of likely and unlikely candidates.

Man's dream of endless social and sexual variety can finally be realized. The illusion of finding the perfect person is enhanced by the concept that there are endless choices on the net constrained only by geography and time.

Some of the realities of internet dating are that men get many more hits than women. Women tend to stay within their age range give or take a few years. Men, on the other hand, may be looking for a woman 20 years younger and up to their age but rarely older. So women are at a disadvantage.

Going on both eHarmony and Match, I found that many more men were available on Match than on eHarmony. Interestingly enough, while both sites make matches for you, none of either the eHarmony or Match matches worked for me. Men who contacted me (or who I contacted) who were not picked by Match nor eHarmony were my best dates and became my best relationships.

You may have lots of dates from one of these services, but many of them may be false starts or one-time dates. This may make you feel either hopeful (that is, you have a way to meet many men) or it may make you feel rejected and result in a loss of confidence. You must make it be the former not the later.

Getting out there and dating requires a strong stomach and a strong ego. If you find yourself feeling rejected, don't give up. Just stop and take a break from dating. Looking at my very attractive friends who have gone through dozens of dates helped me to not take this rejection personally.

In the anonymous market of the World Wide Web, manners can go by the wayside. A meat market mentality can prevail; no need to be polite, there is always another woman/man around the corner and you will never see this one again (maybe.) Relationships are disposable.

Cheating on your spouse or lover has never been easier. In this tempting environment, long, deep, satisfying relationships can be forfeited for variety, novelty and fantasy. So do not be hurt every time someone who seems perfect drops you after a big build up.

A typical man's perspective can be seen in the following statement. A male friend confided, "When you have 400 cable channels, you just keep surfing and surfing. More time is spent surfing than watching. You do not get to really, deeply enjoy any one program…You wind up feeling really frustrated. It is hard not to do that with Internet dating. I was getting 45 hits (new matches) in a month…it was all I could do to keep up with my new contacts."

Cost

Just a warning: the less you pay for a dating site, the seamier things get. Price does seem to add some exclusivity. For example, Craig's List, which is a great resource for many things, has some of the raunchiest personal ads I have ever seen. Most people who want to meet someone of quality will pay to be in a more exclusive group.

Cautions

While opportunities for great new relationships abound on the net, opportunities for disaster are just as easy to step into. Two men gave me these stories:

Mark says: "I had gone on a dating Web site and met a person online who was attractive to me both for her appearance and also her spiritual side. We seemed to have a lot of the same ideals in common.

"I flew to a neighboring state to meet her. She picked me up at the airport and we drove for miles and miles to somewhere in the boondocks. We finally arrived at a compound where she lived. It began to dawn on me that I was trapped in the middle of nowhere, completely at her mercy. We went inside and after chatting awhile, she began to tremble and shake. It seemed like she was in a trance, I was concerned…no, actually terrified. After a few minutes, she came out of it. She told me she had been communicating with her 'angels' to determine if I had the right stuff to be the new leader of her social peace movement. Apparently, I passed the test. I asked—no, begged—to go back to the airport. She seemed disappointed but brought me back. Whew, that was a close one."

Peter had a similar story. He met a woman online who seemed very nice. They chatted back and forth and then arranged to meet at her home in another town about an hour away. When he arrived at her house he realized, "She had substantially misrepresented herself on the Web site." She said that the stars had ordained their meeting. Her sister was there also. They invited him to stay for the night. It was clear that the intent was for him to sleep with one or both of them. "I came up with an excuse and made my escape."

In addition, there are horror stories of women connecting with men online, falling in love and then getting taken to the cleaners financially then abandoned and/or worse.

Honesty Online

To respond to the problem of gross misrepresentation, the states of Florida, Michigan and Texas have passed legislation requiring Internet dating sites to state whether or not they subject potential customers to background checks. The state of New Jersey is also considering legislation to require such disclosures. The law applies to not just online dating services but also to social networking sites like MySpace, Facebook and LinkedIn. If the service does not conduct criminal background screenings on its members, it must say so to all members, clearly and conspicuously, in bold, capital, 12-point letters.[40]

Concerned about honesty online? Anyone can get a background check online with a bit of identifying information. If you have a social security number you can get just about everything.

Whatever you do, remember safety is first and safety is everything. So don't give out your home number, real name and address too quickly. When you go on a first date, always meet in a public location and let a friend know where you are going.

Final Advice

Three friends of mine added this on internet dating:

Janine said, "If someone creeps you out, drop 'em. Google their name, check sex offender lists, ask last name and address before you meet someone. Absolutely ASK about sexually transmitted diseases. Stay out of chat rooms...bad stuff there."

Daniel said, "Be patient, be positive, do not settle. Most of all know what you want...you may find this out only after meeting and dating for awhile."

Peter's advice: "You can be deadly honest. What an opportunity to clean up your act, clear out all old expectations, assess your story and go from there!"

There are many success stories in the world of internet dating—and yours could be one. As a middle-aged secretary I know who found an attractive, distinguished attorney on Match and married him said, "You must not give up...it just depends on what you think you are worth."

Chapter 23
Is He the One?

"Don't ask what the world needs. Ask what makes you come alive, and go do it. Because what the world needs is people who have come alive." Howard Thurman

Gerri Hale-Cooper, who has managed a divorce recovery program in Richmond, Va., for 15 years said, "You attract who you are. If you are vulnerable, you may have a sign on you that says, 'come, abuse me.' " You may have a terrific need to prove your worth (to your ex-spouse and others.) It is critical to heal yourself before you get into another relationship. Heal issues of self-respect. What happened in the marriage? Were there problems of codependency, self-esteem, sex addiction? Was part of it my responsibility?

Let's say you do want a man in your life. Let's say you are dating someone. Let's say you do not want to be on the path to another divorce. So how do you tell if he is a good guy? First of all, you have to look at this person objectively before your eyes are shaded by the rose-colored glasses of love.

Look at this list of questions and objectively answer them based on what your man has said and done in his past and in the present.

1) Are your values in sync? Do you have the same sense of right and wrong? Does he lie, cheat or steal with others? Even the smallest white lie can tip you off that this person feels it is OK to stretch the truth. Whatever he says or does to others he will feel it is OK to do to you. Small stuff, like changing the label on a grocery item shows you that his ideas of what is right and wrong are gray lines. (And no, you can't change him.)

2) How does he talk about other women? Was his ex-wife responsible for everything wrong with the marriage? Did he not get along with his mother? He may not particularly like or trust women in general. You may be the recipient of that dislike when the honeymoon wears off.

3) Did he cheat on his wife and girlfriends in the past? If so, then he feels this is OK when he is dissatisfied with something in the relationship or when he just needs some variety. You won't change that pattern either.

4) Blame- Is someone always to blame in his life? Does he take responsibility?

5) Under stress, does he lose his temper? Under what conditions and what happens? Verbal outbursts, taking a swing at someone? Throwing things? Again, behaviors do not change…and under the stress of marriage these behaviors can increase.

6) Does he change the deal? When courting was he an "I'll do anything for you" guy? Does he keep his promises to you and others?

7) Does he like the real you? Is it your looks that attracted him? Probably, but will the real you hold him? Does he love little things about you? The way you look disheveled in the morning? The way you scatter your materials all around you when working? These things are either endearing or irritating. If he is irritated with you now in little ways—you leave the water running too long, you leave the lights on—these things may become infuriating to him later.

8) Is he jealous of your friends? Possessive of your time? Not wanting you to grow? Your other interests and friends are paths of growth and support. He should not be threatened by this.

9) Does he want control of you? Where are you going and why? A controlling personality may become an abusive personality later.

10) When angry, does he "hit below the belt"? Does he attack you personally?

All of these are serious red flags. Ignore them at your peril.

Steve Harvey[41] writes that the signs that a man is really in love with you are that "he is tickled by you and wants to do for you. He acts as a protector and defends you from his friends; most importantly, you are first on his list."

And, he emphasizes, if you want a man to respect you, you must not have sex with him until you have known him for at least 90 days. By today's practices that sounds like an eternity, but he is adamant. That thought is shared by other writers on love such as John Gray *(Men are from Mars, Women from Venus.)*

Steve writes that it's important to know where your man is headed and he believes that most of them will tell you if you just ask. He suggests that you find out what your man's short and long-term goals are. What does he think about relationships? Not just yours, but with his relatives, children and friends. Finally, don't be afraid, as the relationship develops, to find out what he thinks about you and what he feels about you.

These questions should give you some real insight into who this person is and in what direction you and he are headed.

Merging: Do You Risk the Bliss?

OK, so you have found "the one" (to replace the other "one"). You want to avoid problems, you want to avoid divorce No. 2 or 3. You are in love again at a time when you thought this would never happen again.

So, if everything is blissful, do you risk it by moving in together? Will your attempt to combine two well-defined lifestyles, perhaps with the addition of other family members, in-laws, children and pets, financial problems, choice of TV shows, meals, traditions, etc., create weight that no fragile, beginning-to-bloom relationship can handle? Will you in your attempt to comingle your life with your beloveds kill the very elements you are trying to solidify?

There is both good and bad news on this subject. The bad news is that, according to the Web site divorcerate.org, about 40 percent of first marriages fail, and 67 percent of second and 74 percent of third marriages end in divorce. The good news is that there are many couples who have found ways to keep the critical elements of love and commitment intact and are enjoying their late in life joint ventures.

The elements that might make a second or third marriage more difficult can include children, step-children, elderly parents, pets, jobs in different locations, child support payments, separate houses you both want to keep, and different lifestyles and habits. Moving in together can bring all of these issues to a head.

Often, couples can handle these by simply either continuing to maintain separate households, creating prenuptial agreements or continuing to date without marriage. Each state has different laws regarding inheritance, marital rights and property. How your marriage will affect you from financial perspectives including alimony payments, social security, taxes, Medicaid and medical costs are all things to be considered and are not covered in this book. But many people overcome all these obstacles by being open-minded and non-judgmental about how things should be done and flexible in the way they work problems out.

Here are some examples and advice straight from the mouths of couples who, by marrying later in life, had more complex situations to work out.

Pat, age 56, met Keith eight years ago. They had both been divorced. They began dating and fell in love. For two years they had a blissful relationship. Then they got married and bought a house together.

Keith said, "Pat did not have any kids and I know she lost her independence in marrying me." He had two teenage girls from his previous marriage and his ex-wife worked weekends. So the children were with him every weekend. As he said, "The kids were not receptive to my getting married again. I had been divorced for five years and not dated very much. They did not welcome Pat."

Pat explained that she tried her best, "I was cooking and cleaning for them, but they let me know right away they did not appreciate it." Pat and Keith did not get to spend quality time on the weekends; their honeymoon lasted only four days because of the girl's schedule. He tried to create one big happy family but that failed. Evenings out and trips were built around the girls' schedules and were subject to change as their mom's work demanded. Pat felt as though she always came second. The only trip Pat and Keith took alone in their five-year marriage was a long, honeymoon weekend in Las Vegas.

Another issue was whose relatives to visit on the holidays. Pat's family was in Michigan and Keith's in Pittsburgh. Because his parents were geographically closer, most holidays were spent with his family. When they did visit Pat's parents in Michigan it could be for only one day because of his need to be back to care for the children.

Pat said," I felt I had lost my own identity completely in the marriage." She finally separated from Keith. They still love each other and are back to dating again. The girls are grown and out of the house. Hopefully, Pat and Keith can repair some of the hurt from their past and rebuild their relationship.

Some families, however, have overcome the hurdles of combining families in a big way.

Sharon met Harvey when she was 28 and he was 40. Harvey revealed to her when they met that he had five children, ages 8-18 and was primary caretaker for all of them. Undaunted, Sharon said, "I should have been afraid, but I was young and did not know any better. I was a supervisor in my office and used to resolving problems. So I just thought I could make this work too."

They never sat down and discussed how it would work. Acceptance by the kids? She said the little ones just wanted to be loved. The oldest girl had moved out and was a little cautious in accepting her but it worked out.

Sharon was the rule setter. "When we married, money was tight and so we had to be careful." Sharon set up rules: everyone had chores and would get allowance for those chores upon completion. Sometimes the kids did not get what they wanted. Holidays? "Well, we have two Thanksgivings, one with my husband's son, his wife and his mother (Harvey's ex-wife), the other with the girls and their families. Flexibility is critical."

Which child did they have the most problems with? "That's easy. The one we had together. After three years of marriage, we had a baby girl." She was the baby of the family and the other kids doted on her. "When she became a teenager—wow! From age 12-14, that was the hardest time of all!" Sharon said they were lucky, but that Harvey's desire for things to run smoothly and her belief that problems can be resolved made it happen.

Some couples sit down and make agreements ahead of time. Cheryl has three grown children and five grandchildren. Davis was a widower with no children. They met in 2006 and finally married in June of 2010. They have different feelings about religion. "She is very involved with her church, me less so, but that's not a big deal."

In combining their two well-established households, Cheryl said he let her move the furniture around any way she wanted and even let her make the choices about what to keep and what to throw away. They also had concerns about the children and how they might impact their household. After much discussion, they made an agreement. They would not let the kids move back into the house they shared together. They might do other things to help them but not give up their combined living quarters. This allowed them to proceed with their marriage plans and they have had no major issues since. Finances? Cheryl said, "He said he would not let me pay for a thing." Amen, Cheryl.

Being flexible and non-judgmental about what your partner needs or wants is key.

Carla and Ken have been married for 10 years. Carla had two sons from a previous marriage and now has four grandchildren. Ken said, "I had a background of complete freedom—a lifer at 40—with no marriages to my credit. Carla came with family responsibilities. I have friends who are very hung up on that 'my freedom, my way' stuff. They are so entrenched in their independence."

He explained he had to learn to be less self-serving and more giving. Carla shares that they dated one year, lived together one year, and then married. She said, "Our eyes were wide open when we finally married. I think that was very helpful."

Carla mentioned another difference many couples have. She likes to dance and Ken doesn't. But he is OK with her going out dancing with her friends. Their view of the children is very different too. "I can forgive my children anything. It's responsibility, not just love. People without kids do not understand, but Ken is very tolerant of my perspectives on the kids."

There were differences too in the way they managed their finances. "Finances are a big area. I have never been comfortable with debt, but Carla, having been a business owner, is comfortable with making loans to take advantage of various opportunities as they occur." Ken and Carla bought a business together and were doing well until the recession hit. They were under tremendous pressure personally and as a couple.

Ken remarked, "Our going into business together was a leap of faith. I respected her ability to run a business and she respected my ability to take her on a white water rafting trip. When the business failed, our mutual respect and trust got us through. It was my part to say 'yes' to the business side, so I cannot blame her."

This kind of emotional maturity kept them together as a couple and as a team and got them through some very tough times. They took responsibility, rolled up their shirtsleeves and are working hard to get back on their feet financially.

More Advice from Couples

Carla: "You should pick your battles carefully. It's give and take. Sometimes you have to accept in the other person what you do not understand." She also suggests that it is a good idea to buy a new place together so it is your place together, not his or yours.

Pat said, "One person is always going to be more dominant, more controlling and that leads to resentment. You must know what those person's expectations are." Keith advised, "Don't expect it to be perfect. It does not have to be." But Ken summed it up best: "The commitment must be there. You can't go through stuff in life without that commitment holding you together. I just don't get these people who when things are tough say, 'Hey I'm splitting.' You have to take responsibility for the bad stuff. Every day I must realize that I put myself here because I wanted to be here and Carla is here because of my decisions."

A Counselor's Advice

Margaret Norman, a licensed professional counselor in Richmond, Va., agrees. "This is a commitment and each person needs a clear understanding of what their partner needs." She suggests having an open discussion on what each person's role will be in the relationship. What are their and your expectations, life directions, goals? How will you handle finances? Most importantly, ask what helps each partner to feel emotionally connected and loved.

Preventing another Divorce

Dr. Joyce Hudson adds this additional comment about one of the biggest problems facing couples in the USA. "Successful marriage takes a time commitment as well as an emotional and intellectual commitment. If you look at the time in your life on a pie chart, you have time for your job, for the kids, for the house, for the yard, for church, etc., but if you don't carve out time for your relationship, what good will the yard or house do you?" One of the biggest problems she sees in her practice is couples' fatigue from too many activities and thus no time or energy for sex or the relationship.

Part VIII
The Future

Chapter 24
Things Can and Will Change

"Be the change that you wish to see in the world."
Mahatma Gandhi

Right after my husband left, when I was in a deep dark, self-pitying place; a well-meaning friend gave me a refrigerator magnet that had the trite saying on it, "Just when the caterpillar thinks it's all over—it turns into a butterfly." I sneered at it at the time. But incredibly, in my case, she and the magnet were right. The only good thing about losing a marriage is the need for growth it imposes on you and the freedom it gives you to achieve that growth. If, as Oprah Winfrey said, "The whole point of being alive is to evolve into the complete person you were intended to be," then divorce can be a catalyst for that evolution.

Some of the things that have made this year wonderful are seeing the most incredible sunrise from the second floor of my son's Colorado home over a stone landscape covered in a layer of pristine snow. I saw a new baby girl in my son's arms. I saw the love between him and his wife. I sent my grandchildren a box at Easter and then again at Halloween, decorated inside and out filled with surprise goodies.

I had the most wonderful summer I can remember since my teen years. I went from beach to beach with a passionate and considerate lover who is willing to try anything and can dance for hours. I have been to Tuscany with my girlfriend and her patient husband who trailed us as we checked out every market stall, art gallery and cathedral, fort and museum we could find. I saw Michelangelo's David in person and up close, and it is as heart-stopping as everyone says it is. I saw Botticelli's *Spring* and *Venus Rising from the Sea*—two of my favorite artworks ever.

And friends—it seems curious to me that I have many more friends now than when I was married. I have gone from the illusion of security within a marriage that, unbeknownst to me was destined to fail, to the utter freedom (and insecurity) of a life on my own. I have gone from being someone who saw the world as a small space around my narrow, married life to someone who now sees a world of limitless people, people who are available to love and be loved by me.

Aging, Divorce and Depression

Now, about aging—it does make a difference. You may have become aware of the fact that you have limited days on this earth. You might, for the first time in your life, be asking yourself how many years do I truly have left? Do I have the time to find someone new, or rebuild a career? The short answer is "yes, probably." But those negative feelings may hold you back or stop you in your tracks. John Steinbeck described it perfectly in his book *The Winter of Our Discontent*. The abiding feeling that things are not going to go well—that in fact, you are in a downward spiral that you did not expect to be in at this juncture of your life. What you expected to have at this stage was a sense of accomplishment, achievement, pride in those accomplishments, love for and pride in your children, a fortifying, strengthening relationship with someone you loved who loved you back and still saw in you all the promise that was there at the beginning.

We all hope and expect that at the end of our life, we will have financial security from a lifetime of work, no worries about where or how you would live and always enough for you and your loved ones, and most importantly, someone to love.

But what happens if that is all swept away in an instant or eroded away over months? What if your resources—physical, emotional and financial— are gone and you are left with a feeling that the hourglass is running out of sand and every day your body is telling you that you may still be able to do the same things for awhile yet but at a heavier cost in practice and pain. This is the situation that can make a divorce an even more telling blow.

You may be 30, 40 or 50 but if you are 60 or over, you know you have reached a major milestone. Particularly for a woman, there is nothing great about it. It marks publicly, that you have entered a whole different realm, the dreaded realm of the definitely, no question about it "senior citizen." This means losses: loss of beauty, loss of ability, loss of prestige, etc. In my case the collateral damage cut wide and deep valleys across the physical, mental and financial reserves of my life.

If you have been left for another person, say, a younger person, it feels even worse. That is verification that your age is a liability. I felt like Sleeping Beauty waking up from a 20-year sleep to find that what I believed in, lived for, was an illusion and that it was too late to do anything about it. My husband had said to me months before he met Melissa that he looked forward to us growing old together. That dream of a companion and partner to face the issues of old age was gone.

I believe that, as my friend Gene said, "Sixty is the new forty" and that is the only way to look at things. The average person who really takes care of himself and does not have bad genes can look forward to living well past his parent's ages.

As Catherine Rountree writes in her book *On Women Turning Fifty*, "Once women pass fifty, if they can avoid the temptation of the eternal youth purveyors, the sellers of unnatural thinness, and cosmetic surgery, they may be able to tap into the feisty girls they once were. And if at adolescence the importance of their own convictions had been reinforced they might at fifty be ready to take on risk, display a newfound vitality and bid goodbye to conventional limitations."[42]

Focus on What You've Got

For several years of my life, I worked with individuals who had experienced traumatic brain injuries from automobile accidents, falls and other injuries. They included college kids en route to fulfilling their dreams, attorneys handling important cases, CEOs who were at the top of their professions and mothers with young children to raise. Their lives were changed forever. They could not continue in school, they could not continue their professions, they felt they had lost everything.

In each case, they wondered why this had happened to them. Had they done something wrong? How could they adapt to losing so much? From my viewpoint these were all random occurrences—as random as if lightening had hit them on a clear afternoon.

Their only chance to have a life was to focus not on what they had lost but what they still had. While they had lost the ability to do 1000 things they could still do 900 others. Those who focused tightly on new goals and accepted their new set of abilities did best. Focus on what you can do well, on the opportunities that are still there—not on what you have lost. Grieving should be a stage, a passage into acceptance that leads to a new start. You need to go forward with no buts, no negative thinking; just full steam ahead into your new life.

It's Not Over Till It's Over

Along this line of thinking, consider the many famous individuals who have appeared to be finished and on the ropes, but who came back strong and even surpassed their previous accomplishments.

Consider Hilary Clinton, who is possibly the most publicly humiliated first lady in history. She came back like a lion with her own run for the presidency and a post as secretary of state. Richard Nixon, who resigned from the presidency in disgrace after Watergate, returned to public life to make significant diplomatic contributions with his trips to China and other countries.

Apple president Steve Jobs retired from the company he founded, only to later regain the helm of his company when it was in trouble. Suzanne Somers, after leaving her hit TV series, floundered until she began writing best sellers about women and hormone replacement therapy. Donald Trump was close to bankruptcy, but by rallying his creditors was able to succeed with the Trump World Tower and Trump Palace.

Montel Williams, at the height of his career and in excellent health, developed multiple sclerosis so painful he considered suicide. He made it his business to found a research center for MS and, on his own, located therapies and remedies that have enabled him to come back strong as a TV personality, writer, speaker and snowboarder.

What You Can Do After 60

Think you are too old to do something remarkable? Take a look at what these people have done at 60-plus. Then stop whining and go for it!

Physician, author and running enthusiast George Sheehan ran his fastest Boston marathon ever at 61.

At age 62, J.R. Tolkien published the first volume of his fantasy series *Lord of the Rings*.

At age 69, Ronald Wilson Reagan became the oldest man ever sworn in as President of the United States.

John McCain ran for President of the United States at age 70.

At age 70, Benjamin Franklin helped draft the Declaration of Independence.

At age 71, Casey Stengel began managing the New York Mets.

Retired mining engineer Ed Whitlock became the first man over 70 to run a standard marathon in under 3 hours (2:59:10).

At age 78, Justice Oliver Wendell Holmes Jr. gave his definition of the limits to free speech.

At age 82, Winston Churchill wrote *A History of the English speaking Peoples* and Leo Tolstoy wrote *I Cannot Be Silent*.

At 85, "Coco" Chanel was the head of a fashion design firm.

Viktor Frankl, whose experiences at Auschwitz lead to his writing *Man's Search for Meaning*, continued to teach until he was 85.

At age 87, Michelangelo created the architectural plans for the Church of Santa Maria degli Angeli.

At age 87, Claude Pepper was the oldest man ever elected to the U.S. House of Representatives.

At age 89 Albert Schweitzer ran a hospital in Africa.

At age 90, Chagall became the first living artist to be exhibited at the Louvre museum and Pablo Picasso was still producing drawings and engravings.

Hulda Crooks climbed Mt. Whitney at age 91.

At age 95, choreographer Martha Graham helped her dance troupe rehearse for their latest performance.

At age 92, Paul Spangler finished his 14th marathon.

At age 93, George Bernard Shaw wrote the play *Farfetched Fables*.

At age 95, P.G. Wodehouse worked on his 97th novel and got knighted.

Ten Reasons

If you are not into accomplishments, here are some reasons why I think you might continue to enjoy life through age 100:

There is always another sunrise and sunset, another autumn with leaves, another snowfall to watch, another spring bursting forth, another summer at the beach, another shooting star shower on an August night, another Luna moth in July, another cumulous cloud, rainbow-filled sky, another balmy night with palm trees swaying, another child laughing with delight.

There is always another great new movie, another haunting melody, another stunning play, another courageous, heroic man, another beautiful girl, another book filled with wisdom, another wonderful restaurant, another stunning art exhibit.

There is always another meeting of two minds, another meaningful glance, another shared laugh, another wonderful smile, another kind act, another deed well done. There is always someone to compete against, a bad guy to beat, a good guy to cheer. There is always someone who needs you.

There are always the small and large fights to be fought and the big battle to be won. There is always something to conquer even if it is only within yourself. There is always a project to be finished, another mark to leave.

There is always something new to be learned, a chance to change and a chance to influence for the better. Every day that you live you can contribute to the goodness and the benefit of the world, so every day you live is of great value to all.

Chapter 25
Visualize What You Want

"You gain strength, courage and confidence by every experience in which you really stop to look fear in the face. You are able to say to yourself, 'I lived through this horror; I can take the next thing that comes along.' You must do the thing you think you cannot do." Eleanor Roosevelt

There was an exercise that Ladies Who Launch required. We each had to visualize what we wanted our future to hold and then write it out as though it had already happened. This exercise is how Phillip Knight, co-founder of Nike began his company. He said, "I closed my eyes, saw how I wanted it to be, then put all my energy into that vision."

So, right now, put down this book, get some paper and write out your dream life as though it already happened.

For example, you may write something like "Jane Smith is now a full time teacher, having gotten her master's degree in Special Education. Her paper on identifying learning disabilities was published to excellent reviews in the *Journal of Elementary Education*. She has just purchased her first home where she and her two children will reside. She is dating a man she met in her master's program and enjoying their life to the fullest. They spent a week in Aruba last month while her mother kept the children for her."

This is fun but not play. You are programming your mind to work toward these goals and it will work toward them, even while you sleep at night.

In my case, I wrote that I became a successful freelancer, wrote a book about divorce that would help others, then married a retired professor and moved to my favorite place on earth, Sanibel Island, Fl. In reality, I have become successful as a writer, I have written a book on divorce, and I am investigating moving to Florida. I am dancing three nights a week and I am dating a very big redneck barbarian who is a lot of fun. So, I have achieved at least part of that dream and will continue working toward the rest.

Chapter 26
My Own Last Chapter

"My karma ran over your dogma." Anonymous

It was three years past our separation. Rob and I communicated very rarely and then only about his niece or some leftover piece of business. One day I received an email from him. The subject line read, *"Heads Up Warning."*

He wrote that he had just ended a relationship with a woman. Not Melissa, some other woman. He described her as crazy and confused. He said, "She just texted me that she has your name and phone number and is going to contact you. Don't speak to her, she is dangerous." My first reaction was shock, then some fear. Did I have something to be worried about here?

But as I thought about it, I became more and more curious. I wanted to know what was going on. What had happened in his life? I had never asked him how things were going with Melissa, if she was still with her husband, if they had plans to marry. More to the point, what could this new woman possibly want to talk to me about?

She did call and I took her call. The voice on the end of the line did not sound crazy. She sounded sad. How can I possibly help you I asked? She said she wanted some resolution to the relationship she had with Rob, she needed answers to questions.

She had moved to his town months before to be near her father who had had a stroke. Then her father died. Following this, she had been in a car accident and could not work. It was a very bad time in her life. She went to an outdoor concert with her son, hobbling on crutches. Rob sat near them and struck up a conversation.

He took her number and they began dating. He was romantic, considerate and caring. She thought she had found a "soulmate." She was swept away and quickly fell in love with him. All of his behavior rang true and I could see it happening just the way she described.

She knew he had a business partner he took trips with, but he had said this other woman was "just a business partner." A few remarks, a few clues and she became suspicious. She found "incriminating documents" in his office, references to recent sexual encounters with Melissa. Places they had gone together.

She was in shock.

She said she wanted to understand Rob. He had told her he had been totally faithful in his 20-year marriage to me and that he and I had mutually agreed to separate. He said that only after we had separated had he become involved with Melissa. She wanted to know if this was true.

I explained it was not and told her the whole story. She thanked me for talking with her, saying she knew it must be a difficult subject that I might not want to go back to. I wished her well, telling her I could understand how hurt and confused she was.

Months later, I learned that Melissa, while keeping her business partnership with Rob, had dumped him as a lover. She said she finally realized she really loved her long-suffering husband.

Chapter 27
Stay True to Yourself

"You are what you love, not what loves you." Charlie Kaufman

So what to do about the unfairness of it all? Your only consolation in this situation is well put by Elizabeth Edwards, wife of presidential candidate John Edwards, in her book, *Resilience*[43]:

"In the end the way to view all that has happened to me is that I did my very best. I felt with every part of me—I loved with the whole of me. I have been true to that sense of what was true and right and clean—maybe others had a better time, more intimacies, more skin pressed against skin, but this life is mine, these children are mine, this home is mine…"[44]

You live your life by your own values, keep your friends and family close, and keep your eyes wide open. Do your best to be the best you can be, but do it for yourself and maybe your kids. When my husband left, I vowed I would show my sons how to handle a disaster like this in your life… and I have.

I hope and pray that you will know that no matter what you have experienced, a new, richer life can be waiting for you. Perhaps not the one you thought you might have but a life with a full complement of joy. You are free to make your own choices now, choices for you and your children if you have them, so ask yourself, "What is it I plan to do with my one wild and precious life?"[45]

Epilogue

I was sitting by the pool at a condo in Florida. I was watching families interact. The American family seems alive and well here. I have been at this pool every day for a month. A new batch of families comes in every week, grandmas, daughters, handsome fathers and sons, babies, new mothers, old poppas…all busy nurturing, teaching, entertaining children and one another. It is the same condo my husband and I were at three years ago when we had that last terrible fight. The one that ended in violence and my telling him, "you will have to leave."

I am with my erstwhile big redneck boyfriend. People smile at us, assuming we are married, and that we have been married for a long time. They say, "You are the cutest couple. How long have you been married?" One man, slapping him on the back said, "I bet you guys have been married 30 years or more, right?"

I am horrified by the awful age reference. If they think we have been married that long, I must look ancient. But beyond that, I don't want to be perceived as married any more. I want to be perceived as free. Free to do whatever I want. I don't want their perception to be reality. But here watching the families interact so well, watching how devoted these partners are to their young (and to their elderly parents) is pleasing to us both.

In a few days my children will come: my two noble, handsome sons; my wonderful daughter-in-law with her bubbly personality; the three granddaughters so exquisite in their innocence and fun; my girlfriends' son who is my "third child;" his long, lean lovely girlfriend; and Susan, my ex-husband's niece. The boys have a paternal interest in her, advising her in the ways of the world (especially the male world) and cleaning up her Facebook pages.

There will be big family dinners with discussions of movies, politics, childcare and jobs. There will be a trip to the Island Cinema to see the latest movie. There will be another group photo on the beach at sunset. The sun will turn the piles of clouds pink and gold, the ocean will be aquamarine in the background.

The little girls will squirm and make faces. The adults will stretch arms around each other and smile with real warmth into the camera's eye, feeling the camaraderie of family. The essence of family is selflessness. Families will continue despite the dark things. Despite selfish affairs, disloyalty, lies, greed, anger, jealousy and grieving, despite the statistics, despite all that—families survive, a good sign for the future of man.

And so, you will survive too. The years will go by, making what you will of them, better years, new successes, new friends and maybe new loves as well. I wish you that with all my heart.

Endnotes

1   Sally Warren, *Dumped*, (Harper Collins) New York,1998, p. 6

2   Suzanne Finnamore, *Split*, (Dutton Press,) New York, 2008

3   Stacy Schneider, *He Had it Coming*, (Simon & Schuster,) New York, 2008

4   *New York Daily News*, from court testimony, 07/03/2008

5   Debbie Reynolds, *Debbie, My life*, (William Morrow), New York,1988

6   M. Gary Neuman, *The Truth About Cheating*, (John Wiley & Sons,) New York,2008

7   Website: http://news.softpedia.com/news/The-Biology-and-Psychology-of-Cheating-85610.shtml

8   Website: http://social.jrank.org/pages/202/Divorce-Divorce-Rates-Demographics.html">Divorce—Divorce Rates And Demographics

9   *"Life's Short,Get a Divorce"*, billboard, sponsored by Fetman, Garland & Associates, Ltd, Chicago Law Firm, May 2007.

10   Website: http://www.gallup.com/poll/107380/cultural-tolerance-divorce-grows-70.aspx

11   Louise DeSalvo, *Adultery*, (Beacon Press,) Boston, 1999, p. 116

12   Julie Metz, *Perfection*, (Harper Collins,) New York, 2009.

13   *Esquire*, March 2010, anonymous essay, http://www.esquire.com/features/reasons-why-men-cheat-0410#ixzz10mL0gyrS

14   Steve Harvey, *Act Like A Lady, Think Like a Man*, (Harper Collins,) New York, 2009, p. 39

15   Steve Harvey, *Act Like A Lady, Think Like A Man*, (Harper Collins,) New York, 2009, p. 107

16   Steve Harvey, *Act Like A Lady, Think Like A Man*, (Harper Collins),New York, 2009, p. 94

17   Website: http://www.truthaboutdeception.com/

18   Dr. Joyce Ann Hudson, Ph.D., Licensed Clinical Psychologist, Richmond, VA

19   Interview with Dr. Joyce Ann Hudson, Ph.D. Richmond, VA

20   Ivana Trump, *The Best is Yet to Come*, Simon & Schuster, New York, 1995, p. 54

21 Stacy Schneider, *He Had it Coming*, (Simon & Schuster,) New York, 2008

22 Ivana Trump, *The Best is Yet to Come*, (Simon & Schuster,) New York, 1995, p. 54

23 Mary Jo Buttafuoco, *Getting It Through My Thick Skull*, (Health Communications, Inc.,) Deerfield Beach, FL 2009

24 Sally Warren, *Dumped*, (Harper Paperbacks,) New York,1998, p.108

25 *Chicago Personal Injury Lawyer's Guide*, http://www.chicagopersonalinjurylawyerguide.com/divorce-lawyers-speak-out-on-common-mistakes.htm

26 Gerald Nissenbaum, *Sex, Love & Money: Revenge and Ruin in the World of High-Stakes Divorce,* (Hudson Street Press,) New York, 2010

27 Website: www.divorceremedy.com

28 T. Harve Eker, *Secrets of the Millionaire Mind: Mastering the Inner Game of Wealth*, (Harper Collins,) New York, 2005

29 *Yale Journal of Biological Medicine*, 1988 May-Jun;61(3):259-68.*Suicide attempts in the Epidemiologic Catchment Area Study,* Mo cicki EK, O'Carroll P, Rae DS, Locke BZ, Roy A, Regier DA., Division of Clinical Research, National Institute of Mental Health, Rockville, MD, 20857.

30 http://www.metanoia.org/suicide

31 Olivia Goldsmith, *First Wives Club*, (Simon& Schuster,) New York,1992

32 Anne Newton Walther, *Divorce Hangover*, (Tapestries Publishing,) San Francisco, 2001

33 Dr. Bruce Fisher with Dr. Robert Alberti, *Rebuilding*, (Impact Publishers,) Atascadero, CA, 2006

34 Website : http://fbcrichmond.org/recovery/index.htm

35 Dr. James Carraway, Virginia Beach, VA, website: http://www.evmshealthservices.org/index.cfm/fuseaction/site.physicians/action/dtl/phys/99853768.cfm

36 Sally Warren, *Dumped,*(Harper Collins,) New York, 1998, p. 220

37 *Act Like A Lady, Think Like a Man*, Steve Harvey, (Harper Collins ,) New York, 2009

38 *The Secret Psychology of How We Fall in Love*, Dr. Paul Dobransky , (Penguin,) New York, 2007

39 Dr.Diana Kirschner, *Love in Ninety Days*, (Center Street,) New York, 2009

40 Michael Booth, *Internet Dating Law, The Legal Intelligencer*, ALM Media, Nov. 30,2007

41 Steve Harvey, *Act Like a Lady, Think like a Man*, (Harper Collins,) New York, 2009, p. 117

42   Cathleen Rountree *On Women Turning Fifty*, (Harper,) San Francisco,1993, p. 1

43   Elizabeth Edwards, *Resilience*, (Broadway Books,) New York, p. 78

44   Elizabeth Edwards, *Resilience* (Broadway Books,)New York, 2009, p. 149

45   *The Summer Day*, poem by Mary Oliver

Manufactured by Amazon.ca
Bolton, ON

27549282R00101